"My childhood dream was to one day become a 'godly old lady.' At the time, that goal didn't seem particularly daunting. Now that I'm in my sixties, it sometimes feels like climbing Mount Everest. Always a few steps ahead of me, Susan Hunt has encouraged and inspired me to press on in my journey. She has also been a spiritual 'grandmother' to the True Woman ministry since it launched. She has given us all a vision of flourishing in old age, for the glory of God and the good of his people. In this book, Susan and Sharon Betters have teamed together to provide perspective, wisdom, and hope for women coming behind them. They call us to keep our eyes on Christ—the prize—and to persevere to the summit, dependent on his grace every step of the way."

Nancy DeMoss Wolgemuth, author; Founder, Revive Our Hearts and True Woman

"Some women seem to grow increasingly lovely with every year that passes. I want to learn from women who display that type of beauty and grace. That's why I'm so thankful for *Aging with Grace*. This book is a wealth of wisdom for women of all ages to learn from God's word the secret of aging with grace—I highly recommend it!"

Melissa B. Kruger, Director of Women's Initiatives, The Gospel Coalition; author, *Growing Together: Taking Mentoring beyond Small Talk and Prayer Requests*

"As I embark on my seventh decade, I find myself saying things about 'finishing well,' while at the same time moaning about the aches and trials that are my unbidden companions. But one of the gifts I love most are the friends who are walking with me. Sharon Betters and Susan Hunt are two of those friends. Let me encourage you to join them as they encourage you to walk through the final steps of your journey with faith and joy. They have encouraged me."

Elyse Fitzpatrick, author, *Worthy: Celebrating the Value of Women*

"As a woman on the cusp of her forties, I've harbored a secret fear of aging. More than the changes of my physical appearance, I've feared becoming obsolete as I age. I read *Aging with Grace* with a lot of tears and thankfulness as my fears were turned to praise. Sharon Betters and Susan Hunt address the realities of aging with biblical encouragement to fix our gaze on our timeless God who will finish the work he started in us. Because God is faithful, our growth in Christ will continue as we age. This is a book I will return to over and over again."

Glenna Marshall, author, *The Promise Is His Presence* and *Everyday Faithfulness*

"Seasoned with wisdom, *Aging with Grace* offers us the biblical recipe for a life marked by hoping in Christ. Through examples of women in the Bible as well as women in the church today, Susan Hunt and Sharon Betters guide us to reflect on God's faithfulness to his people throughout all of redemptive history, reminding us that it's never too late to sink our roots in the soil of God's word for his glory and our good."

Hunter Beless, Founder and Executive Director, *Journeywomen* podcast

Aging with Grace

Flourishing in an Anti-Aging Culture

Sharon W. Betters
and Susan Hunt

CROSSWAY®

WHEATON, ILLINOIS

Library of Congress Cataloging-in-Publication Data

Names: Betters, Sharon W., 1948– author. I Hunt, Susan, 1940– author.
Title: Aging with grace : flourishing in an anti-aging culture / Sharon W. Betters and Susan Hunt.
Description: Wheaton, Illinois : Crossway, 2021. I Includes bibliographical references and index.
Identifiers: LCCN 2020013771 (print) I LCCN 2020013772 (ebook) I ISBN 9781433570070 (trade paperback) I ISBN 9781433570087 (pdf) I ISBN 9781433570094 (mobi) I ISBN 9781433570100 (epub)
Subjects: LCSH: Christian women—Religious life. I Aging—Religious aspects—Christianity. I Older persons—Religious life.
Classification: LCC BV4527 .B4925 2021 (print) I LCC BV4527 (ebook) I DDC 248.8/5—dc23
LC record available at https://lccn.loc.gov/2020013771
LC ebook record available at https://lccn.loc.gov/2020013772

"The righteous flourish like the palm tree
and grow like a cedar in Lebanon. . . .
They still bear fruit in old age;
they are ever full of sap and green."

Psalm 92:12, 14

Contents

To our husbands,
Chuck Betters and Gene Hunt, who
for decades have shown us the way
of righteousness, and now daily show
us the way of aging with grace.

To our friends who open their hearts
and share their stories in this book:
Carol Arnold, Ruth Auffarth,
Dianne Balch, Pam Benton, Sherry Bitler,
Jerdone Davis, Judy Didier, Jane Patete,
Lynda Tedeschi, and Barbara Thompson

We are grateful for your transparency
in showing us the brokenness of
flourishing, and your hope, which shows
the beauty of flourishing. Your stories
supremely show that aging with grace is
impossible apart from God's grace.

Foreword

KAREN HODGE

*Women's Ministry Coordinator,
Presbyterian Church in America*

When do you start to finish? Today is the day!

Inside every older woman is a little girl trying to figure out who she will be when she grows up. We long to flourish and thrive, not just in old age but right here and now. When I was twenty-nine and struggling with this question (and, by the way, I still am), Susan and Sharon entered my life. I watched and learned the shape of godliness from their lives. I can testify after serving alongside them twenty-plus years that they are still "full of sap and green" (Ps. 92:14). Now they have written what they have learned about aging with grace. This is the book I need now, and it's the book I want to give to younger women.

Are we promised tomorrow? Today is the day!

The word of God describes life like a mist or a blade of grass (Ps. 103:15). Our season for flourishing is fleeting and temporal, but eternity is forever. Living in light of eternity impacts not just us, but our children's children. "But the steadfast love of the LORD is from everlasting to everlasting on those who fear him, / and his righteousness to children's children, / to those who keep his covenant / and remember to do his commandments" (Ps. 103:17–18). The pages of this book remind us to begin with the end in mind, that our reference point for life is God, and that his word is our authority. "The grass withers, the flower fades, / but the word of our God will stand forever" (Isa. 40:8).

Do you desire to flourish to the finish? Today is the day!

Remember my friends, we are not running this race alone. We are surrounded by many who were faithful to the finish. Run with the women Sharon and Susan introduce us to in this book. They will disciple you to lay aside the life-taking thinking and actions that encumber you. Run with women in your church by studying this book together and helping one another divert your gaze from the worldly anti-aging culture and fix your eyes on Jesus. (A leader's guide is available.) Start running, sister, and run until we get home (Heb. 12:1–2)!

> Only one life 'twill soon be past.
> Only what is done for Christ will last.[1]

Now join me in a conversation with Sharon and Susan.

———

Karen Hodge: When did you start thinking about aging?

1 Attributed to missionary C. T. Studd.

Sharon Betters: My husband, Chuck, was twenty-one when he became pastor of a small church. Because my childhood pastor's wife taught a Bible study, I thought I should too. Every week five elderly women sat at our table and let me teach them. Who did I think I was? Yet they loved and encouraged me, listening as though I knew what I was doing. They were life-givers. But there were also a couple of elderly women who scared me with their sharp tongues and criticism of my husband's preaching and leadership. They were life-takers. All of these women were rooted in the church, yet not all of them offered kindness and love. That's when I started my quest to understand God's view of aging and how I could intentionally prepare to be the sweet, life-giving old lady who encouraged young women just starting out in life.

Susan Hunt: I think my obsession with thinking about being an older woman was largely due to my passion for and commitment to the Titus 2 mandate that older women "are to teach what is good, and so train the young women" (Titus 2:3–4). I wondered when I would be an older woman. Now, my aging body assures me I am one, and I love the perspective from this season of life.

Karen: What prompted you to write about aging?

Sharon: Even though we are both older women—I'm seventy-two and Susan is eighty—it's doubtful either of us would have thought about writing this book. However, a workshop I was asked to teach on purposefully preparing for old age resonated with older and younger women. I laughed when some of them asked me to write a book.

Susan: When Nancy DeMoss Wolgemuth asked me to speak on the Titus 2 older woman for a True Woman conference, I was shocked at the response from women of all ages. Sharon and I began discussing the question, "What does God say about aging?" We studied Scripture and prayed. Between us we have forty-two children and grandchildren (including spouses). We were compelled to write what we learned for our generation and theirs. It feels outlandish to write about ending well when we haven't ended, but we do not write only about what we have experienced; we write about what God's word tells us. We are awestruck by his calling and promise for this season of life.

Karen: Why do you believe our culture is anti-aging?

Sharon: American culture idolizes youth and measures value by what a person produces for society. When older people stop contributing financially through working, show signs of wear and tear, and slow down mentally and physically, culture considers us worthless. Some see the elderly as a drain on society. Why wouldn't I dread aging when I have been trained to chase after youth and do everything I can to slow down the inexorable march into old age? Unless we are purposeful in fighting the throw-away, anti-aging messages with a biblical worldview, we will face this season with fear, dread, and denial.

Susan: Secular psychiatrist Carl Jung first coined the phrase "the afternoon of life" and defined it as fifty-six to eighty-three years of age. He said: "Wholly unprepared, we embark upon the second half of life. Or are there perhaps colleges for forty-year-olds which prepare them for their coming life and its demands as the ordinary colleges introduce our young people to a knowledge of the world?"[2] To answer Jung's question, the world cannot prepare us because it has no hope or power to give us. Culture's false narrative about aging is the church's opportunity to proclaim the hope and power of the gospel to equip God's people to flourish even in old age.

Karen: How do you approach the topic in this book?

Susan: Our approach is very simple—we asked the Lord to teach us how to glorify him as older women, we studied the Scriptures, and we share some of the things we learned. We alternate; I write a chapter on *Thinking Biblically* about aging using Psalms 92 and 71, then Sharon writes a chapter on *Living Covenantally* in old age. This was an interdependent endeavor. Our ideas flowed into each other's work, our voices became one in our desire to "glorify the God and Father of our Lord Jesus Christ" (Rom. 15:6).

Sharon: Throughout Scripture we often see an explanation followed by an example. The *Living Covenantally* chapters are

2 *The Collected Works of C. G. Jung,* vol. 8, *Structure & Dynamics of the Psyche,* ed. and trans. Gerhard Adler and R. F. C. Hull (1969; repr., Princeton, NJ: Princeton University Press, 1981), np.

examples of the explanation in the *Thinking Biblically* chapters. We don't consider ourselves experts on aging with grace, so we selected older women in Scripture who illustrate the principles in Susan's chapters. I soon knew I was on holy ground. I often paused and whispered, "What am I missing? Tell me your story. Let me get inside your skin and show me the treasures hidden in your soul." I am forever changed by getting to know these matriarchs better, and we pray you will be too. They show us what aging with grace looks like and how this is not an independent endeavor—it happens in community with God's people.

Karen: Is there a prevailing theme you do not want readers to miss?

Sharon: Yes! We want readers to truly believe that the Bible gives us not only the promise of bearing fruit in old age, but it also gives us a road map to grow and flourish in this grace. We want readers to ask, "What if aging, though challenging, is not a season of purposelessness, but rather an opportunity to discover our true identity in a way we couldn't in the first half of life? What if we purposefully prepare for the afternoon of life while we are in the first half of life?" And for those already in the afternoon of life— perhaps ill-prepared, feeling worthless, and rudderless—we want them to know it's not too late to experience God's grace and, through his work, make an eternal impact in this season of life.

Susan: Our point is that aging with grace, or what the Bible calls growing in grace, is impossible apart from God's grace.

When the disciples asked Jesus, "'Who then can be saved?' . . . Jesus looked at them and said, 'With man this is impossible, but with God all things are possible'" (Matt. 19:25–26). This book is not a list of ideas to become a gracious older woman. It's about the life-long adventure of God giving his children the desire and ability to do all things—even aging with grace—through him who strengthens us (Phil. 4:13). We have no nifty formulas to give you. Actually, there is nothing new in this book; but we don't need anything new. God has given us the means of grace—his word, prayer, worship, sacraments, fellowship—to grow in our relationship with him. And he says to us, "Stand by the roads, and look, / and ask for the ancient paths / where the good way is; and walk in it, / and find rest for your souls" (Jer. 6:16). So come walk the ancient paths with us as we explore God's promise and provision for aging with grace.

Sharon: We asked some of our friends who are at least seventy to tell their stories. We are confident their stories will disciple you, as they have us, to age with grace. Their stories embody the message of this book, so we offer two of them to read before you begin chapter 1.

Ruth's Story

Ruth Auffarth partnered in ministry with her husband, Bob, for over forty-six years, most of that time in Newark, Delaware. She has three children, thirteen grandchildren, and four great-grandchildren. Hundreds of women claim Ruth as their spiritual mother. She was widowed at seventy-three.

I'm eighty-eight years old and live in Gainesville, Georgia. In this season of life, flourishing means being overwhelmed by the difference between my "receivings" and my "deservings," as an old Puritan observed.[3] Looking back on my life, I see God's sweet hand of providence again and again. Each day is a gift. Now that life has slowed down, I have more time to study the Scriptures, and oh, how much more precious that time has become. God's thoughts jump off the page with encouragement and joy that can be applied to the exact situation I am facing. Early mornings on my porch I pray, "Satisfy us in the morning with your steadfast love, / that we may rejoice and be glad all our days" (Ps. 90:14).

In praying for family and friends I confidently ask, "Make us glad for as many days as you have afflicted us, / and for as many years as we have seen evil" (Ps. 90:15).

Yes, the days of affliction come. Part of flourishing is fervently grabbing hold of the Lord through his promises. He says, "Draw near to God, and he will draw near to you" (James 4:8). Gladness comes with his presence. As you grow older, expectations change. You come to realize that there is no perfect family, church, situation, or society. Because we live in a broken world, we begin to marvel that things go as well as they do because God gives grace upon

3   Arthur Bennett, *The Valley of Vision* (Carlisle, PA: Banner of Truth Trust, 1975), 12.

grace. We look for his intervening hand of love as we work through difficulties. Struggling and rejoicing can happen at the same time as we let the struggles bring us closer to God's warm embrace.

Another gift God gives for our flourishing is the local church. Active participation in a shared faith makes us a real family as we worship, sing, pray, serve, rejoice, and sorrow together.

We find joy when people respond to the gospel. After years of teaching Bible studies, I now attend several women's studies as a student, where I find younger women are hungry to hear from an older woman. The Lord also gives me the privilege of counseling at the local crisis pregnancy center.

Finally, I am focused on God's promise that "surely goodness and mercy shall follow me / all the days of my life, / and I shall dwell in the house of the LORD / forever" (Ps. 23:6).

Dianne's Story

Dianne Balch and her husband, Dave, spent forty-four years establishing various lay ministries nationally and internationally. While they were in New York, she directed the women's ministry at Redeemer Church. She has two children, six grandchildren, and two great-grandchildren.

I began the year with a month of reflection. Advice from forty years ago, when I faced a life-shattering trial, resurfaced; "Don't look back, except to thank God for what he has pulled you out of or brought you through. Then ask, 'What am I going to do with what I have left?'"

As I reflected, I remembered.

When Dave was diagnosed with inoperable lung cancer, we prayed the prayer that never fails: "Thy will be done." God gave us peaceful hearts, and Dave arrived in heaven seven months later. We were passionate partners, crazy in love. After fifty-four years of marriage, I grieved deeply, and I worshiped more deeply than ever before.

When my colon cancer surgery and recovery were heaped onto ten years of Chronic Lyme Disease, I prayed for strength to trust the Lord with *all* my heart. I grieved the loss of independence, but I knew the peace of his presence with me.

When I pondered how long I should remain in a home, church, and community I loved, I prayed, "As I approach seventy-nine years, is it time to make my twenty-fifth move and go to another state?" My month of reflection produced clarity only God and his word can give. It's time. *Let go.*

So I've let go of teaching the Bible after forty-five years, leading women in evangelism and discipleship efforts, "Titus-twoing" with teens through eighty-somethings, and loving all of it.

I've let go of my home, furniture, and keepsakes, and moved west, only to return two months later to my southern community and church. The Lord led me through a trial to see where I belong and why. Weary after months of letting go, I've shed tears, counted blessings, and known Jesus's presence and comfort. It's been hard, but I've found freedom; I have been sorrowful but always rejoicing (2 Cor. 6:10).

My reflections also reminded me of what I will *not* let go—trusting God's promises that Christ is in me, his grace is sufficient, and his power is made perfect in weakness, and praying for unsaved or suffering family and friends.

So what am I going to do with the time I have left? My answer is the same as it was forty years ago—*make it count.* Only the Lord who directs my path knows what that will look like. I may flounder, but he is faithful. Oh, how I love Jesus!

A Note from the Authors

From Sharon

Prolonged church conflict, life-threatening breast cancer, loss of our sixteen-year-old son Mark. Add to these the care of our family and life as a pastor's wife. Jesus wasn't joking when he said, "In the world you will have trouble." The Lord did not put me in a sweet cocoon of grace during these dark times; I often wrestled to reconcile his love with his sovereignty.

Here's the good news. Jesus finished his dire warning in John 16:33 with this promise: "Take heart; I have overcome the world." He did not reject me when I struggled to trust him, but instead held me tightly in his grip, where I experienced unconditional love and learned to trust him once more. I experienced his faithfulness in ways I never thought possible. I wrote this book out of the context of years of experiencing Jesus's overcoming grace in my life. Your story may be similar or different, but I pray this book will encourage you to trust his overcoming power, no matter what path he calls you to walk. May we look forward to arriving home—where we will fully experience the victory won by King Jesus.

From Susan

A few weeks after this book was submitted to Crossway, my beloved husband, Gene, died. He was sick for only about three months, and until the last few days we thought he would recover. He was a vibrant, active, joyful man. His life was a celebration of the power of the gospel. Seeing him lying in a hospital bed, getting weaker by the day, was shocking; but it was a sweet and sacred journey as our children, grandchildren, and I were with him to his final breath on this earth. It is important to me for you to know this book did *not* flow out of that context. This book was completed before Gene's home-going. Writing this book was God's gift to prepare us for this season of suffering and sorrow. I don't think it would have occurred to me in the fog of fatigue and uncertainty to think about either of us flourishing, but I had learned from Psalm 92 that the righteous will flourish, even in old age. My prayer for both of us was shaped by this promise.

So as you read this book, my friend, I want you to know I can now put big exclamation points on every page. God's grace is sufficient, and his grace is specific. When it's time to age, he gives aging grace. When it's time to suffer, he gives suffering grace. When it was Gene's time to die, the Lord gave dying grace. And now he is giving me grieving grace.

———

An *Aging with Grace* Leader's Guide with lesson plans may be ordered from:
1-800-283-1357
www.pcacdm.org/bookstore

1

Wonder and Worship
Psalm 92:1–4

SUSAN

Our granddaughter Suzie was about four when she slid down the stairs on her pillow just as her mother rounded the corner and saw her. Thus began the following conversation:

"Suzie! Don't ever do that again!"

"Did you do this when you were a little girl?"

"No, my mother wouldn't let me."

"Who is your mother?"

Surprised she did not know this, her mom answered, "*Memommie* is my mother."

Without flinching Suzie replied, "No, she's not. She's an old lady."

Suzie is now twenty-four, which makes me a very old lady. But here's the thing: I have been happily married for fifty-six years, have three children, twelve grandchildren, and one granddaughter-in-love. You *have* to be an old lady to have these amazing blessings.

The world tells us aging is our enemy, and we should fight it; the Bible says it's our friend: "Wisdom is with the aged, / and understanding in length of days" (Job 12:12).

Let's be real—aging doesn't feel very friendly. Change is disorienting, because we settle into our roles and responsibilities and they become our identity and purpose. And now we face almost daily changes of diminishing physical abilities and energy. We need something bigger and better to make sense of it all. We need an identity and purpose that transcends it all, which is exactly what God provides in the gospel.

The gospel is big enough, good enough, and powerful enough to make every moment of every season of life significant and glorious. The one who created us promises we can flourish and bear fruit, we can be full of sap and green, even in old age (Ps. 92:12–14). These lively words indicate growth and vitality. They seem to contradict my reality as an eighty-year-old who suffers with inflammation of the connective tissue in my body that causes pain and weakness in my muscles. But this promise of growth does not mock my physical reality; it transcends it.

The gospel imperative to "grow in the grace and knowledge of our Lord and Savior Jesus Christ" (2 Pet. 3:18) does not have an age limit. The same grace that gives us new life in Christ empowers that life to develop, mature, and flourish. We never finish growing. There is always more grace to experience and more to know of Christ's love. This growth is gradual. We don't produce it, but as we trust and obey God's word, we can anticipate it.

We had almost finished writing this book when I fell, damaging muscles in my neck and jaw that caused severe headaches. My kind doctor told me. "*At your age* this will take a couple of months to heal." I spent many days lying in a dark room, sometimes wondering what it would mean to age with grace if I never got better. I prayed, "Lord, what does it mean to flourish and be fruitful right now when I do not feel like doing anything?" I reflected on Psalm 92, and prayed that he would make me glad (92:4). Some days I fought fears and fatigue, but I began to realize I was not afraid. I was content, and I knew Jesus was with me. I thought, "This is not wasted time. It is growing time, because my physical weakness and pain push me to trust Jesus more. My heart is full of an ineffable gladness." Honestly, I'm shocked by that statement. The only explanation I can give is the one Jesus gives to Paul: "My grace is sufficient for you, for my power is made perfect in weakness" (2 Cor. 12:9).

So let's walk the timeless and timely path of Psalm 92 with expectant hearts, eager to know how to flourish and be fruitful as long as we live in these earthly bodies.

Psalm 92:1–4

A Song for the Sabbath

> [1] It is good to give thanks to the LORD,
>> to sing praises to your name, O Most High;
> [2] to declare your steadfast love in the morning,
>> and your faithfulness by night,
> [3] to the music of the lute and the harp,
>> to the melody of the lyre.
> [4] For you, O LORD, have made me glad by your
>> work;
>> at the works of your hands I sing for joy.

The title of Psalm 92, "A Song for the Sabbath," indicates this is a communal song that was used in the context of worship. Notice how Sinclair Ferguson connects flourishing to worship:

> It is at the end of life, not only at the beginning, that Christians are most different from the rest of the world. Then the true beauty of a woman, the true character of a man, is seen for what it really is. That is why there sometimes seems to be a touch of glory and light about the lives of elderly Christians. They have remained "fresh and green" as Psalm 92 suggests, because their hearts have been given to the Lord in worship. . . . True worship puts character into our lives, humility into our bearing, strength and confidence into our witnessing. . . . Let us learn to worship God, with the faithfulness and joy of the author of Psalm 92.[1]

---

1 Sinclair Ferguson, *A Heart for God* (Edinburgh, UK: Banner of Truth Trust, 1987), 116–17.

The psalmist's unbridled joy in God is contagious. His God-centeredness is compelling.

What is the first thing that comes to your mind when you think about God? Our answer is one of the most important things about us because it reveals the arc of our life. It determines the choices we make and shows whether we understand that our identity is not based on what we do but on who we are in Christ. The psalmist leaves no doubt that his knowledge of God is not a product of his imagination or his circumstances; it is the product of God's revelation of himself in his word.

GOD REVEALS HIMSELF THROUGH HIS NAMES

Note the two names the psalmist uses in Psalm 92:1.

LORD is the English translation of the Hebrew word *Yahweh*. This is God's personal, covenant name whereby he reveals himself to us as the covenant-making, covenant-keeping God who enters into a personal, forever-relationship of love with his people. His covenant is his marriage bond with his chosen ones. The very mention of *Yahweh* immediately reminded the elderly Israelites that the Lord never stopped loving or pursuing them, even when they sinned. For us, on this side of the cross, this name brings an even fuller understanding of never-ending covenant blessings, which include:

- God's covenant plan that began in eternity past when the Father chose us in Christ and predestined us for adoption through Christ to the praise of his glorious grace (Eph. 1:4–6);

- His covenant promise in Genesis 3:15 that he will rescue us from Satan's bondage by providing an off-spring of the woman who will crush Satan's head;
- His repetition of this promise throughout Scripture: "I will be your God, you will be my people, and I will live among you" (see Gen. 17:7; Ex. 6:7; Deut. 29:10–13; Jer. 24:7; Zech. 8:8; 2 Cor. 6:16; Rev.21:3);
- The fulfillment of the promise when "the Word became flesh and dwelt among us, and we have seen his glory, glory as of the only Son from the Father, full of grace and truth" (John 1:14);
- The victory of the promise when the crucified Christ rose triumphantly from the grave, conquering sin and death. "Thanks be to God, who gives us the victory through our Lord Jesus Christ" (1 Cor. 15:57);
- The provision of the promise when the resurrected Jesus said, "I am with you always, to the end of the age" (Matt. 28:20);
- The expectation of the promise when "every knee should bow, in heaven and on earth and under the earth, and every tongue confess that Jesus Christ is Lord, to the glory of God the Father" (Phil. 2:10–11).

"O Most High" is the English translation of the Hebrew word *Elyon*, another name for God, which describes the sovereignty, majesty, and transcendent glory of our Creator and sustainer.

These two names show that the psalmist knew the familial nearness of God as his Father and the stunning transcendence of God as his King. These names bring together the themes of covenant, creation, fall, redemption, restoration, and consummation. This is the big story that holds every moment of our story together.

We are all products of our theology. What we believe, or don't believe, about God shows up every day. Sound theology produces sound thinking and living. As we face the sorrows and physical suffering of aging, thinking biblically about who God is and who we are in Christ comforts and carries us. God's word accomplishes his purpose in us (Isa. 55:10–11).

Growing in Grace

God reveals himself to us in his word. Our flourishing happens in proportion to time spent getting to know him through his word. An ever-growing knowledge of God produces a more mature, God-centered perspective on our identity and purpose, which are the same in every season of life.

IT IS GOOD

These first three words of Psalm 92 echo God's declaration at the close of each creation day (Gen. 1), reminding us of the rhythm of work and worship established by our Creator when he "blessed the seventh day and made it holy, because on it God rested from all his work that he had done in creation" (Gen. 2:3). God's people now gather on the first day of the week to celebrate Jesus's resurrection—his triumphant victory over sin and death—and to anticipate the everlasting Sabbath rest "for the people of God" (Heb. 4:9).

The psalmist tells us, "It is good to give thanks" (Ps. 92:1). The apostle Paul also exhorts those who are in Christ to "rejoice always, pray without ceasing, give thanks in all circumstances; for this is the will of God in Christ Jesus for you" (1 Thess. 5:16–18).

We don't necessarily give thanks *for* all things but rather *in* all things—in every situation and relationship—we can "give thanks to the LORD, for he is good, / for his steadfast love endures forever!" (Ps. 106:1).

Growing in Grace

As we move through the various seasons of life, the steady rhythm of weekly corporate worship is one way we regularly stop and unite our voices with others to give thanks to the Lord for his amazing grace. This helps to develop the grace of gratitude, which is a means and evidence of flourishing.

MORNING AND EVENING DECLARATION

In Psalm 92:2, the psalmist tells us it is good to begin and end each day by declaring God's steadfast love and faithfulness. "Steadfast love" (from the Hebrew word *hesed*, sometimes translated "lovingkindness") is a rich, multifaceted concept. Sinclair Ferguson writes:

Hesed [is] one of the "big" words in the Old Testament Scriptures. It appears around 250 times, and dominantly with reference to God himself. He is a God of loving-kindness. . . . When God revealed himself to Moses, he said that he was a God full of *hesed* (Exodus 34:6)—not simply love or kindness in an ordinary sense. It means God's deep goodness expressed in his covenant commitment, his absolute loyalty, his obligating of himself to bring to fruition the blessings that he has promised, whatever it may cost him personally to do that.[2]

It cost God his Son. It cost the Son his life. Jesus embodied *hesed*.

We see the triune God's unrelenting faithfulness to his covenant of redemption when the first man and woman committed cosmic treason against him. He could have ended it all, but because he had chosen a people in Christ before he created the world, he pursued the man and woman. They were hiding, but he was seeking; and he still is: "The Son of Man came to seek and to save the lost" (Luke 19:10). He promises, "I have loved you with an everlasting love; / therefore I have continued my faithfulness to you" (Jer. 31:3). Our sin can never out-distance God's steadfast love and faithfulness. But the question is, How do we continue in faithfulness? Jesus tells us, "Abide in me, and I in you. As the branch cannot bear fruit by itself, unless it abides in the vine, neither can you, unless you abide in me. . . .

---

2 Sinclair Ferguson, *Faithful God: An Exposition of the Book of Ruth* (Bryntirion, UK: Bryntirion Press, 2007). 64.

Whoever abides in me and I in him, he it is that bears much fruit, for apart from me you can do nothing" (John 15:4–5).

The repetition of declaring the gospel to ourselves gradually becomes the melody of our soul. Faithfully declaring God's *hesed* in word and deed develops a pattern of remaining constant even in changing circumstances. It is what Jesus called abiding—remaining, continuing, staying, enduring, submitting.

Growing in Grace

Our bodies change as we age; so do our spirits. We must guard against our hearts becoming brittle and bitter by praying for grace to abide in Christ and bear the fruit of steadfast love and faithfulness to others, even when it is costly.

GLADNESS

This exuberant statement is extraordinary: "You, O LORD, have made me glad" (Ps. 92:4). We look for gladness in people, things, and circumstances, and we are always disappointed. Even if gladness comes, it is temporary. We don't usually connect gladness and worship. Sometimes people say, "I don't like the worship at that church." What does that even mean? Worship is not something we observe and critique; it is something we *do*. In fact, *it is what we were created to do*. And in doing it, the psalmist found great joy. The answer to the first question of the Westminster Shorter Catechism captures this understanding of life.

Q. What is the chief end of man?

A. Man's chief end is to glorify God, and to enjoy him forever.

When Moses was in the desert with a stiff-necked congregation (God's description, not mine, Ex. 33:3), he prayed. Two of his petitions were "Show me now your ways, that I may know you" and "Show me your glory" (33:13; 18). The only thing that could make sense of Moses's situation was knowing God and seeing his glory. God replied: "I will make all my goodness pass before you" (33:19). Then God hid him in the cleft of a rock and passed by, proclaiming the goodness of his own glorious character: "The LORD, the LORD, a God merciful and gracious, slow to anger, and abounding in steadfast love [*hesed*] and faithfulness, keeping steadfast love for thousands, forgiving iniquity and transgression and sin." And Moses's response? He "quickly bowed his head toward the earth and worshiped" (Ex. 34:6–9). The result? "Moses did not know that the skin of his face shone because he had been talking with God" (Ex. 34:29).

Moses's circumstances did not change, but Moses changed. He grew in his knowledge of God's character, he worshiped, and he reflected God's glory to stiff-necked people. When I was recovering from my fall, Gene's care of me continually reflected the goodness of God to me. Shortly after I recovered, Gene was hospitalized. Yes, we felt we were getting a crash course in aging. As Gene needed constant care, not knowing whether his circumstances would change, his reflection of

God's character became brighter. Even talking was exhausting, but he never failed to show kindness to our children and me, to the doctors and nurses, and to all who cared for him. He thanked us for what we did, and he always spoke of God's goodness. Whether he was giving or receiving care, his worship and reflection of his Savior never wavered. It grew. One especially difficult day our son was caring for his dad. When I thanked him for his tenderness, he responded, "It stretched me, but I kept thinking of all Dad has done for me through the years." Ah—isn't that the way it works? As we think of the Lord's goodness to us, we become good, and we become glad.

Will we be stiff-necked or shining old ladies? As we spend time listening and talking to God, we slowly know him better, we know our identity as his children, and we gradually become like our Father. "Those who look to him are radiant, / and their faces shall never be ashamed" (Ps. 34:5).

Proverbs 16:31 tells us, "Gray hair is a crown of glory; / it is gained in a righteous life." Gray hair is a sign of age. The crown is the reward for righteous living. I am not one of those women with beautiful gray hair that does indeed look like a crown, but this is not about hair color, is it? It refers to the reflected glory of the one who lives face-to-face with Jesus, seeking to know him better each day. One of my spiritual daughters calls it *the gospel glow*.

Our primary calling is to glorify God. All other callings are extensions of that. Our calling to be a daughter, employer, employee, wife, mother, single mom, widow, or old lady, our calling to serve others or to suffer, is a calling to glorify God in that relationship or situation. The venue changes, but the calling remains the same. Often when a woman retires from her vocation or after her children leave the home, she feels useless because her purpose was centered on what she was doing rather than what she was becoming. The calling to glorify God transcends place, time, circumstance, and age.

Growing in Grace

There are many things we can no longer do as we age, but age does not keep us from fulfilling our purpose to glorify and enjoy God. An ever-growing knowledge of God's undeserved love—his grace—changes our motivation: "The love of Christ controls us" (2 Cor. 5:14). When our prayer is that his love for us will increasingly compel us to stop living for ourselves and to live for his glory, we will age with grace.

WORSHIP

Notice the psalmist's involvement in worship in Psalm 92. He gathers with God's people to hear the preaching of God's word, gives thanks, sings praises, and declares God's love and faithfulness. And God makes him glad. God is glorified when we are grateful and glad, because he is the source of these graces.

Charles Bridges, a nineteenth-century pastor in the Church of England, wrote, "Again and again must we be reminded that every motion must begin with God. . . . The secret of Christian energy and success is a heart enlarged in the love of God."[3] So we pray:

> Love divine, all loves excelling, Joy of heav'n, to earth
>   come down:
> fix in us thy humble dwelling, all thy faithful mercies crown;
> Jesus, thou art all compassion, pure, unbounded love
>   thou art;
> visit us with thy salvation, enter ev'ry trembling heart.
>
> Finish, then, thy new creation; pure and spotless let us be:
> Let us see thy great salvation perfectly restored in thee;
> changed from glory into glory, till in heav'n we take our
>   place,
> till we cast our crowns before thee, lost in wonder, love,
>   and praise.[4]

Growing in Grace

The more we know the triune God, the more we rejoice in our identity as his child and our purpose to glorify him. This knowledge results in worship that is transformative. God makes us glad. God fills us with joy. And this gladness and joy, this wonder and praise, do not diminish with age; they increase until we take our place in heaven.

I was in my late forties when my husband went on staff of a church with many righteous, radiant older women. Several

3   Charles Bridges, *Psalm 119: An Exposition* (1827; repr., Carlisle, PA: Banner of Truth Trust, 1974), 78.
4   Charles Wesley, "Love Divine, All Loves Excelling," 1747.

of them had attended and faithfully served that church all their lives. These women had watched their farmlands become neighborhoods and their rural church fill up with new people. They never resented these changes, and they lovingly welcomed the strangers among them. They flourished as they made us feel like family, and so did we. One of these women was Evelyn, who was in her eighties.

One day I visited Evelyn and poured out my heart to her. I was overwhelmed with life. I whined and grumbled. She listened and never interrupted me or rolled her eyes at my self-centered immaturity. Finally I asked, "What do you think I should do?" She was quiet for a few moments and then lovingly spoke life-giving words that soothed my soul. "As you talked, I kept thinking of one thing—Jesus loves me this I know, for the Bible tells me so."

Evelyn did not criticize me. She did not give me solutions. Her life and lips declared the steadfast love and faithfulness of Jesus based on the authority of his word. She did not minimize my story by telling me her story, but I knew her story and it gave tremendous weight to her words. Her mother died when she was four years old. Her daddy moved in with his mother, who cared for Evelyn and her three siblings, including her brother Ralph, who was mentally challenged. Before the grandmother died, she told Evelyn, "Take care of Ralph." Evelyn's husband died when she was sixty-three. She never had children, but she took care of Ralph, and she had a host of spiritual children.

Until she was bedridden in an assisted-living home, Evelyn was in Sunday school and church every Sunday always looking fresh and beautiful. Her gray hair was a crown of glory that was gained in a righteous life (Prov. 16:31). She lived to be a hundred. She discipled me until she died, not by her words, because the time came when she could not speak, but by her grateful submission to God's word and his plan for her life.

How do we age with grace? Psalm 92:1–4, along with Evelyn's life and words, shows me that a worshiping, grateful heart becomes a glad heart that glorifies and enjoys God. The opposite is also true. A grumbling heart becomes a sad heart.

Lynda's Story
Lynda Tedeschi is a retired registered nurse and interior decorator. She has three children and seven grandchildren. She has taught women's Bible studies and lives in Newark, Delaware.

I was thirty-nine when my husband died of a rare lung cancer. It had been a difficult marriage because he had years of undiagnosed endogenous depression, but before his death God healed our relationship. I'm grateful for our last year together and that he is with his Savior.

Today I am almost seventy-five and married to a godly man, but soon I will be alone again. Andy has mesothelioma and is in hospice care. When I heard his diagnosis, I cried,

"Again, Lord?" My stepdaughter gently responded, "God prepared you to take care of my dad." And she was right.

Since the death of my first husband, Jesus has shown me through his word the depth of my need for him and the sufficiency of his grace. Before I only understood saving grace; now Jesus has made living by grace a reality.

I survived my first marriage and the death of my husband by my own strength, repeatedly telling myself, "You can do this!" My heart was full of self-righteousness, pride, and a determination to survive on my own. Now, as I watch Andy die, I admit I am incapable of doing this alone; I need Jesus.

How does one flourish when the love of her life is dying? When Andy heard there was no treatment left to fight his disease, he exuded peace, knowing he would soon be with Jesus. As I slid into the abyss of disappointment and grief, terrified by the idea of life without my dear husband, I also felt the strong arms of Jesus holding me tightly. I soon realized flourishing in this place requires me to daily die to self. Every morning I wake up, not knowing if this will be my last day with Andy, and sorrow floods my soul. Then I fall at the feet of Jesus, knowing I cannot do this apart from his grace. Because I know him better, I rest in him, and the peace that passes all understanding washes away my fear. Jesus began a work in me many years ago, and in this season of life I am being completed in my suffering so I can minister to others who may be suffering. For now, God has called me to love and care for my husband. Because of Jesus, I will not just survive this; I will flourish as I walk with Andy to the edge of heaven.

Questions for Reflection and Discussion

1. What do you learn about abiding in Christ from the following?
   John 15:1–11
   John 8:31–32
   1 John 2:3–6, 28
   1 John 4:13–16

2. Read Exodus 33–34.
   a. In 33:18–19, when Moses asked to see God's glory, what did God say he would show him?
   b. Make a list of the words God uses in 34:6–7 to describe his goodness. Ask the Holy Spirit to transform your character so you reflect these characteristics to others.

3. Which *Growing in Grace* principle is especially helpful to you at this point in your life and why?

2

Anna
Luke 2:25–38

SHARON

A pastor once asked an elderly, childless widow, "What can I do for you?" Her simple response: "Don't forget me."

I heard the same cry in my widowed eighty-four-year-old mother-in-law's words as we settled her into a rehab center. She was recovering from surgery for a broken leg and was unable to care for herself. I asked her to describe her concerns about her new surroundings. She responded, "I'm afraid you are going to leave me here and forget about me." We shared tears as I tried to convince her we would never, ever do that. Her altered mental state diminished her ability to grasp the reasons for her temporary home. The only reassurance she could cling to was that I had never lied to her before. In her weakened condition, she had to choose to trust my assurances that we would never neglect or forget her. Perhaps this is one of the greatest fears of everyone, but the elderly are especially vulnerable to such fear. We want to know that at least one person in this world remembers us, cares for us, protects us, sees us, and will not forget us. We want the presence of another. Our Father meets this deep need with the promise of his presence, the essence of the covenant promise: "I will be your God, you will be my people, I will dwell among you" (see Jer. 7:23; 31:33; 32:38, Ezek. 37:23).

Did Anna whisper the words, "Oh Lord, don't forget me"?

Anna pops into the birth narrative of our Savior and then disappears just as quickly, but Luke's description of this powerful encounter paints a picture of a holy woman who hoped in God.

Other than Mary and Joseph, only four individual Israelite names are connected to the miraculous birth of Jesus. At least three, possibly all four, are elderly. Old Zechariah and Elizabeth experience their own miracle in the birth of John, Jesus's cousin. After the birth of Jesus, when Mary and Joseph take him to the temple at the time of purification, God lovingly encourages them through Simeon (his age is not certain but the context implies he is older) and Anna, who is eighty-four. Their age did not stop them from hoping in the promise of the Messiah or from glorifying him as they waited. God's choice of including elderly people in the narrative underscores his perspective on aging:

Wisdom is with the aged,
>   and understanding in length of days. (Job 12:12)

Gray hair is a crown of glory;
>   it is gained in a righteous life. (Prov. 16:31)

Anna's Story

[25] Now there was a man in Jerusalem whose name was Simeon, and this man was righteous and devout, waiting for the consolation of Israel, and the Holy Spirit was upon him. [26] And it had been revealed to him by the Holy Spirit that he would not see death before he had seen the Lord's Christ. [27] And he came in the Spirit into the temple, and when the parents brought in the child Jesus, to do for him according to the custom of the Law, [28] he took him up in his arms and blessed God and said:

[29] "Lord, now you are letting your servant depart in
>   peace,
>   according to your word;
[30] for my eyes have seen your salvation
>   [31] that you have prepared before the face of all
>   peoples,
[32] a light for revelation to the Gentiles,
>   and for glory to your people Israel."

[33] And his father and his mother marveled at what was said about him. [34] And Simeon blessed them and said to Mary his mother, "Behold, this child is appointed for the fall and rising of many in Israel, and for a sign that

is opposed [35] (and a sword will pierce through your own soul also), so that thoughts from many hearts may be revealed." (Luke 2:25–35)

God's people had waited for centuries for the fulfillment of the promise. Who would have expected the big reveal in the temple to be a poor couple and a baby? Notice the pervasive providence of God choreographing every detail of this event. Everyone showed up and their lives intersected at the right time and the right place. Reflect on the wonder of this reality in your life.

How often do we miss God's treasures because we don't recognize the little things as the big things?

How do we know these intimate details of such a private moment? Many years later an older Mary is Luke's source, so reading this passage is like reading her personal journal. Imagine Luke writing as fast as he can as Mary steps back into this joyful and terrifying time. All those confusing and mysterious moments Mary had pondered in her heart stream out of her lips. Details that didn't make sense at the time come together in a beautiful tapestry, each colorful stitch a treasure in the darkness sent to Mary by her heavenly Father. I suspect this scene replayed in Mary's mind many times, especially at the foot of the cross when "the soldiers pierced his side with a spear" (John 19:34) and the sword in her soul went deep. But the sure hope that her redemption was being accomplished went even deeper.

Simeon told Mary the hard reality that a sword would pierce her soul. Can you sense Mary holding her baby boy a little tighter, her throat constricting and tears welling up? This young mother needed a tangible touch of God's tender love. At this intense moment we meet eighty-four-year-old Anna. God providentially met Mary's need through an old woman who hoped in God. At exactly the right moment, Anna shows up.

Luke's comments about Anna are packed with information, but they are also short on details of Anna's life. Filling in some of the blanks requires speculation based on other Scriptures. Before looking at the encounter in the temple, let's get to know Anna.

PLANTED IN THE HOUSE OF THE LORD

[36] And there was a prophetess, Anna, the daughter of Phanuel, of the tribe of Asher. She was advanced in years, having lived with her husband seven years from when she was a virgin, [37] and then as a widow until she was eighty-four. She did not depart from the temple, worshiping with fasting and prayer night and day. (Luke 2:36–37)

What prepared Anna, a single, elderly woman, to be a life-giver to Mary, a young girl just starting out as a wife and mother who has been told that mothering this baby will bring a sword to her soul? More importantly, what prepared Anna to recognize and welcome Jesus as the Messiah?

The rhythm of Sabbath worship was probably part of Anna's Jewish family legacy since her infancy. Perhaps the repetitive singing of the psalms, including Psalm 92, seared God's promises into her heart.

We can assume Anna dreamed the same dreams as other Jewish girls. She expected to marry and raise a family in a close-knit ethnic community. Instead, seven years after marriage, her dream shattered when her husband died. Her options as a young widow were few. The death of her husband in the Jewish patriarchal culture resulted in economic, social, and cultural upheaval.

Traditionally, sons took care of their widowed mothers. Since Anna lived and served in the temple, we can assume she was barren, or her children had died, or her children neglected her. Each of these is reason for grief. Anna was vulnerable and alone. What hope did she have? How many times did she cry to the Lord, "Don't forget me. Give me hope that you will keep your promise; give me the comfort of your presence"?

Anna was widowed. Her hope for a husband was broken.

She was childless. Her hope for children was broken.

She depended on others for protection and provision. Her hope for security was broken.

When Anna was widowed, we do not know whether she immediately turned to the Lord and his people or whether she forgot the promises. Sometimes the journey through suffering is long and dark. Sometimes the distractions and despair are overwhelming.

Whether it was immediately or much later, at some point Anna began to think biblically, which prompted her to live covenantally. Perhaps she remembered Scriptures that tell us God loves widows (Ps. 68:5–6) and actually becomes a husband to them (Isa. 54:4–5). His word repeatedly instructs his people how to care for widows (Ex. 22:22–23; Deut. 24:17–21). In time, hopeful words from Scripture, planted in her heart like tiny sticks of dynamite, exploded into comfort and guidance. Anna turned to the Lord and his people. Perhaps the words of Psalm 92:1–4 that had been buried in her heart began to sprout and blossom.

ANNA THE AGED

³⁸ And coming up at that very hour she began to give thanks to God and to speak of him to all those who were waiting for the redemption of Jerusalem. (Luke 2:38)

We meet Anna about sixty years after the death of her husband, and we meet her in the house of the Lord, the place God had planted her. Theologians agree that Anna might have moved into the temple, but it's also possible she lived in an alms apartment close by. Luke's description of her as worshiping night and day is a summary statement of her life in old age; Anna abided in the promise of the coming Messiah.

Anna had reason to despair, but at some point she chose to learn what it means to worship in the darkness. Only one hope could sustain Anna over the sixty years since the death of her husband—the hope that God would indeed keep his promise to send the Messiah. Worship in response to the suffering in her life prepared Anna to see Jesus when others did not; she knew him. Choosing worship with tears streaming down her cheeks cultivated that seed of hope, and it grew into a flourishing, fruit-bearing elderly woman. R. C. Sproul describes our unbroken hope this way:

> Our divine vocation is not ultimately to suffering, but to a hope that triumphs over suffering. It is the hope of our future inheritance with Christ. This hope is no mere wish or idle longing of the soul. It is a hope that is rooted in the exceedingly great power of God. It is a hope that cannot fail. For those who embrace it, this hope will never bring shame or disappointment. The hope of eternal joy in the presence of Christ, a hope that sustains us in the midst of temporary suffering, is the legacy of Jesus Christ. It is the promise of God to all who put their trust in him.[1]

At eighty-four years old Anna is in full bloom.

She was a prophetess. She declared God's word. She spoke of redemption—the gospel story. She recognized the Messiah. She saw majesty in what others would call mundane. She gave thanks. The grace of gratitude was her immediate response. She lived covenantally. She knew God's people and spoke about Jesus to those who were waiting for him. She lived generationally. She spoke life-giving words of hope to the young woman with a sword in her soul.

---

1   R. C. Sproul, *Surprised by Suffering: The Role of Pain and Death in the Christian's Life* (Lake Mary, FL: Reformation Trust), 134.

Anna chose to see widowhood as her platform to glorify God.

What does it look like to worship instead of despair? My sister, Jane Anne, tells this story about our sister Gayle:

> Gayle's husband passed away just five weeks after a cancer diagnosis. Shortly after his death, we spent Thanksgiving with Gayle and her family. We were sitting at her big dining room table making plans for the Thanksgiving dinner and working on a guest count. She counted up the total, and we all realized she had inadvertently added her husband. No one wanted to tell her. When she realized it, she burst into tears, slammed her fist on the dining room table, and declared loudly, "God is good." That was her grid. Whatever else happens, God is good, and therefore we have hope.

Anna and Us

Anna's story parallels our own. As we grow older each day, circumstances confront us with a choice. Will hopelessness or unbroken hope take up residence in our hearts? Will hope stir us to sing with those who have gone before us, "For you, O Lord, have made me glad by your work; / at the works of your hands I sing for joy" (Ps. 92:4)? Will we live with the anticipation that one day, through death or the coming of Jesus, each of us who belong to him will experience that same incredulous joy when our hope becomes a reality and we see Jesus? Will we wait with frustration, or will we abide in Christ?

You may view retirement as your best years. You may have more disposable income and time. Your bucket list calls your name, and you can't wait to start experiencing all the things you had to put on a back burner when you were working hard to succeed in the first half of life. Yet, there is a nagging feeling you might be missing something. You want your life to be significant, and you want to leave an imprint in the hearts of those you love.

Or you may be looking at this season of life and wondering how you're going to survive the losses, the changes, the empty house, the loneliness, the lack of purpose. You feel useless because what gave you value in the first half of life no longer satisfies or is no longer there.

Whatever your age, it's not too late, or too soon, to flourish. One of the ways we can prepare or even adjust our course is to intentionally consider our view of aging and how that view impacts the daily choices we make.

The Bible is my authority for faith and life, including how I view aging. This means when life starts spiraling out of control, God's word should be the road map that determines how I respond. Having said that, I often struggle to make a biblical worldview my first response. Aging is one of those areas where I have to choose to review what Scripture teaches about growing old. Someone has said, "Everyone wants to live a long time, but no one wants to go through the aging process." I am one of those who want to live a long time, but challenges of old age sometimes frighten me. It's imperative that we allow God's word to guide, comfort, and prepare us for this journey.

Let the repetitive use of the word *nowhere* in the following quote emphasize the critical need for us to think biblically about aging:

> *Nowhere* in the biblical canon are they [the elderly] pitied, patronized or treated with condescension. *Nowhere* is growing old itself described as a problem. *Nowhere* are elders described as pitiable, irrelevant or behind the curve, as inactive or unproductive. *Nowhere* are they, as in so many Western dramas and narratives, lampooned as comic figures.[2]

Nowhere does God diminish the value of the elderly. In fact, he showcases the beauty he sees in aging. Our view of aging, no matter what our season of life, determines whether we value the elderly and whether we recognize our value in the last season of our lives.

Pastor Tim Challies values and learns from the older members of his congregation. He writes:

> I recently spent a little bit of time with an older believer. . . . I was touched by the most mundane observation: She was reading her Bible. She was reading her Bible so she could better know and serve her God. This simple act touched and challenged me.

2   Richard B. Hays and Judith C. Hayes, "The Christian Practice of Growing Old: The Witness of Scripture" in *Growing Old in Christ*, ed. Stanley Hauerwas, Carole Bailey Stoneking, Keith G. Meador, and David Cloutier (Grand Rapids, MI: Eerdmans, 2003), 11. Emphasis added.

See, I often read my Bible as a means to an end. . . . I want to live a life that is pleasing to God, and I read the Bible to teach and equip myself to do this. . . .

As I sat with this woman, I realized that she was reading her Bible for a different reason—she was reading her Bible to better get to know the God she would soon meet face-to-face. . . . She knows she will be seeing him soon, and she wants to be prepared. . . . She is not passively waiting to see him face-to-face but meeting him now in the pages of his living and active Word. She believes that what she knows of God on this side of the grave will not end at the grave. . . . She has the rest of eternity to grow in her relationship with God. So why not make a significant beginning now?

So yes, I need to read God's Word to live a life that is pleasing to God. But I also need to read God's Word to know the God I will enjoy for eternity. What I learn about God is not just for this life. . . . It is for forever.[3]

A final word about Simeon and Anna: Are you amazed they each showed up in the temple at just the right moment? It may be stretching the point, but it seems worth noting that when we are led by God's Spirit as they were, we will move in the same direction—we will move toward Jesus. We will recognize, worship, and glorify him together. We will marvel at the wonder of him. And then we will move toward those who need a reminder of his presence with them. And get this:

---

3 Tim Challies, "Learning for Forever," *Challies.com* (blog), April 1, 2016, challies.com/articles/learning-for-forever/.

old age does not hinder this sacred movement. Rather, the challenges of aging are our opportunity to know, enjoy, and glorify God.

Jane's Story

Jane Patete lives in Chalfont, Pennsylvania, and has two children and six grandchildren. She is the former Women's Ministry Coordinator for the Presbyterian Church in America.

As a young child I looked forward to the changing seasons. My parents and grandparents taught me to delight in God's glorious creation, and the Lord continues to grow my wonder, purpose, and delight in the changing seasons of my life. My life was chosen in Christ before the foundation of the world that I should be holy and blameless before him (Eph. 1:4)

At age sixty-eight God took me into a deep valley. My dear mother was called home. Ten months later, the Lord called Tom, my beloved husband of forty-seven years, home suddenly. Amid grief and uncertainty, God was my faithful Comforter, enveloping me in his loving presence and truth. He surrounded me with the body of Christ to help me navigate the challenges and decisions I faced. The weekends were some of my loneliest days in those early months, as I replayed the times we shared. One Saturday, I prayed for the Lord to direct my steps—that I would be a good steward of my day. I found myself walking through Target, enjoying being with people. I eventually made my way to the dressing room, where the woman in charge said, "Honey, I have been watching you smile, help, and enjoy your time here, and I am thinking you have the joy of the Lord in you." We had a sweet moment as we spoke of our mutual love for Jesus and even managed a brief hug and prayer. That seminal encounter has shaped my walk and opportunities as a child of God in this season.

My days were soon filled with the challenges of saying good-bye to the home my husband and I had loved for twenty years, a home that had resounded with joyous memories of our children, six grands, and many guests. I saved cleaning our library until last. As a former librarian at Westminster Theological Seminary, I considered it my favorite room. I loved the spiritual wealth of it and made plans to box up many of the treasured volumes to share with seminary students and pastors.

In my seventy-fifth year, my roots hold firm in Christ. These ensuing years point to his faithfulness and comfort in and through me as I seek to be a faithful prayer warrior and encourager to my grands who live nearby and to my new covenant body. Each new day offers a sovereign calling to live my joy before others (Ps. 71:17–18).

Questions for Reflection and Discussion

1. Why do you read the Bible?

2. Summarize your understanding of a biblical view of aging. Compare your view of aging with a biblical view. How is it different? The same?

3. Describe one event in your life where you can now see how God was working to advance his kingdom in your heart and to prepare you to encourage others.

4. Anna embraced her widowhood as her platform to glorify God. What difference could Anna's perspective make in your attitudes, reactions, and choices each day?

3

Destiny and Destination
Psalm 92:5–11

SUSAN

I was in my early fifties when I heard a pastor speak about seeing many Christians become bitter and withdrawn in old age, and of his desire to see them finish strong. His message took root in my heart, and I began praying for grace to finish well. But honestly, this is not an easy discipline. I forget. I become immersed in the dailiness of life—good and hard things—and I do not stay focused on my destiny or my destination. I slowly absorb the messages of an anti-aging culture.

The dictionary defines *destiny* as "the predetermined, usually inevitable or irresistible, course of events" and "the power or agency that determines the course of events."[1] Synonyms are *fate, fortune, luck, karma, chance, providence, predestination, divine decree, God's will*. Ironically, these synonyms reflect two conflicting worldviews.

The world tells us to determine our own destiny. The Bible tells us God chose us in Christ before creation to put his glory on display (Eph. 1:4–6), that "those whom he foreknew he also *predestined* to be conformed to the image of his Son" (Rom. 8:29), and he even determined the time in history and place on the planet for us to fulfill our predestined destiny (Acts 17:26). Our destiny to reflect God's glory is based on the authority of God's word; it is truth, not luck.

Our *destination* is the place we are going.

The world gives a plethora of options to believe about our destination. The Bible gives two: "The wages of sin is death, but the free gift of God is eternal life in Christ Jesus our Lord" (Rom. 6:23). Jesus is preparing a home for those who are in him, and at the appointed time he will gather us to live with him (John 14:1–3).

Psalm 92 does not blur these worldviews. The second stanza of this Sabbath Song gives the compelling contrast—a typical teaching technique of Hebrew poetry—between the destiny and destination of those who worship God and those who do not.

I sometimes hear Christians, especially older people, say, "I'm okay under the circumstances," or, "I'm hanging in

1 Dictionary.com, s.v. "destiny," https://www.dictionary.com/browse/destiny?s=t.

there." I am not minimizing their sorrow and suffering, but "under" and "hanging" are not the destiny of God's people.

Martyn Lloyd-Jones wrote:

> The more I try to live this Christian life, and the more I read the New Testament, the more convinced I am that the trouble with most of us is that we have never truly realized what it is to be a Christian. If only we understood what the Christian really is and the position in which he is placed, if only we realized the privilege and the possibilities of that position, and above everything, *the glorious destiny* of everyone who is truly a Christian, then our entire outlook would be completely changed. . . .
>
> There are only two groups of people in the world today—those who are of the world and those who belong to Christ. . . . In light of this, it is vital that we should ask ourselves the question: Am I of the world or am I not?[2]

Psalm 92:5–11

> [5] How great are your works, O LORD!
>   Your thoughts are very deep!
> [6] The stupid man cannot know;
>   the fool cannot understand this:
> [7] that though the wicked sprout like grass
>   and all evildoers flourish,
> they are doomed to destruction forever;
>   [8] but you, O LORD, are on high forever.

---

2 Martyn Lloyd-Jones, "Not of the World," in *O Love That Will Not Let Me Go*, ed. Nancy Guthrie (Wheaton, IL: Crossway, 2011), 35–36 (adapted from Lloyd-Jones's *The Assurance of Our Salvation* [Wheaton, IL: Crossway, 2011]). Emphasis added.

⁹ For behold, your enemies, O LORD,

for behold, your enemies shall perish;

all evildoers shall be scattered.

¹⁰ But you have exalted my horn like that of the
wild ox;

you have poured over me fresh oil.

¹¹ My eyes have seen the downfall of my enemies;

my ears have heard the doom of my evil
assailants.

This stanza pushes us to answer the question, Am I of the world or am I not? If we belong to Christ, we are exiles in a foreign land, but Peter reminds us we are *elect* exiles, and that changes everything (1 Pet. 1:1). These verses help us know *how* to age with grace as we live with the earthly realities of being elect exiles in an anti-aging culture.

Created to Know God

Verses 5–6 of Psalm 92 contrast those who know Yahweh and those who do not. This is not talking about our mental capacity. The word "stupid" here is a translation of the Hebrew word for *brutish*. James Boice explains:

According to the Bible, men and women are *made to know and enjoy God*, but when they turn their backs on God, as the unregenerate do, they isolate themselves from all that is spiritual in life and operate on a physical level only. . . . *It is man's calling to look up to God and become like God, in whose image he is made.* But if he will not look up, the only place he will be able to look is down, and he will begin to behave like an animal.[3]

We are made to know God. Jesus said, "This is eternal life, that they know you, the only true God, and Jesus Christ whom you have sent" (John 17:3). What an astonishing idea—I can *know* God! Even more astonishing, *he knows me* and has a plan for me.

> I know the plans I have for you . . . plans for welfare and not for evil, to give you a future and a hope. . . . I will restore your fortunes and gather you . . . I will bring you back to the place from which I sent you into exile. (Jer. 29:11, 14)

The more we understand that God has a *plan for us*, and he will *gather* us to himself, the more we flourish.

The grand mystery of God's plan of redemption "is Christ in you, the hope of glory," and Paul wants us to *know* this hope so we will be "mature in Christ" (Col. 1:27–28). The hope of glory is future, but there are very real implications right here and right now. Our union with Christ results in a radical change from beast to beauty.

Have you heard older people say, "I'm too old to change"? That is *not* thinking biblically; it is isolating our thinking from all that is spiritual. News flash—just as

3 James Montgomery Boice, *Psalms*, An Expositional Commentary (Grand Rapids, MI: Baker, 1994), 2:757. Emphasis added.

surely as our bodies change, so do our hearts. The question is, Am I becoming beautiful like Christ, or am I becoming brutish? We are continually confronted with this choice. Jesus made provision for us to choose beauty: "The glory that you have given me I have given to them, that they may be one even as we are one, I in them and you in me" (John 17:22–23).

His glory is in us *now*. His glory is the essence of who he is. This glory empowers us to actually live in relationship with one another and reflect the beauty of his glory to each other—his mercy, graciousness, slowness to anger, steadfast love and faithfulness, and forgiveness (Ex. 34:6–7).

When our hope for glory is anchored in Jesus, our circumstances and relationships don't necessarily change, but there is a radical change in our character, attitudes, and actions. Sinclair Ferguson describes what this change looked like in the psalmist:

> This ordinary man becomes someone extraordinary as he praises God. He becomes poet, chorister, composer, musician, theologian, all in one! . . . What has happened to him (and what happens to us in worship) is that he has discovered his destiny. He was made for this, as the famous first question of the *Westminster Shorter Catechism* says: . . . "Man's chief end is to *glorify* God, and to *enjoy* him for ever." It is only when we are restored to God, and begin to worship him, that instead of falling short of his glory through sin (Rom. 3:23), we begin to

66

see his glory, by grace, and bow joyfully and willingly before him.[4]

It was an older woman who helped me understand how this change happens. I was a young mother trying hard to be a Proverbs 31 woman, and I was continually frustrated with the failure of my efforts and the lack of cooperation of my people. Over and over I heard Lillian joyfully say, "I did what I wanted to before I was a Christian. I do what I want to do now. God has changed my *want-tos*." Slowly I stopped trying to manipulate and control the sanctification of others, and I began to ask the Lord to change my heart and help me reflect glory to others. I began to rest in him to accomplish his purpose in my life and the lives of others in his time.

Growing in Grace

Old age, when life becomes quieter and slower, is prime time to reflect on the power of the gospel to change us. It is also a time when we are tempted to think small—to think about our aches and pains, our disappointments and unrealized expectations. Will we be good stewards of our old age? Even as physical strength diminishes, will we pursue our destiny—knowing God? We are never too old to look up and be transformed from beast to beauty, without Botox or anti-aging cream.

---

4 Sinclair Ferguson, *A Heart for God* (Edinburgh, UK: Banner of Truth Trust, 1987), 112.

Look Up

Until we get to our heavenly destination, we will find our-selves easily distracted with the mundane routine, the trials and tribulations of living in a fallen world, and the frustration of our own sinfulness. We struggle to look up to God and become like him. Ask Peter.

In Matthew 14 Jesus "made the disciples get into the boat" and go to the other side (v. 22). They were exactly where he sent them when a raging storm beat upon them. Jesus went to them, walking on the wild water, and said to them what he says to us: "Take heart; it is I. Do not be afraid" (14:27). Peter asked for permission to get closer to Jesus, and Jesus said, "Come." Peter fearlessly got out of the boat and walked on water. Then it happened. His eyes wan-dered, and so did his heart. He looked down at the wind and waves and began sinking. Then he remembered. He looked up and called to Jesus, and "Jesus immediately reached out his hand and took hold of him" (14:31). Even though he walked on top of the water for only a few moments, they were moments of intimacy with Jesus; they were flourishing moments.

I was with my daddy the last three days of his life. Shortly before he took his first breath in heaven, he opened his eyes wide, and with a look of wonder he raised his hand and pointed up. "Look!" he exclaimed. His arm fell to the bed and his eyes closed. "What? What did you see, Daddy?" I asked. His voice was weak but joyful, "You can't see it." I could not see what he saw, but one day I will. This memory reminds me to look up.

Growing in Grace

As long as we live in this world, we are prone to look down. The rhythm of Sabbath and daily worship recalibrates our minds and hearts in the present moment to remember our destiny and destination while "waiting for our blessed hope, the appearing of the glory of our great God and Savior Jesus Christ" (Titus 2:13), when we will experience the ultimate change—glorification.

Gathered

Psalm 92:7 describes those who look down and flourish like grass. After a few days of blazing heat with no water, grass withers; its flourishing is temporary. Where we look determines what we worship, and what we worship determines what we become. "Those who make [idols] become like them" (Ps. 115:8). This is the destiny of those who do not know God. And their destination is destruction. But we are elect exiles and "God has not destined us for wrath, but to obtain salvation through our Lord Jesus Christ" (1 Thess. 5:9), so the psalmist points us to Jesus, who is our hope for a future.

Psalm 92:8–11 presents the gospel. When we study Scripture, we should always drill down until we see the hope of the gospel. The horn of an animal is a symbol of power; it is a weapon. Scripture refers to Jesus as the "horn of salvation" (Ps. 18:2; Luke 1:68–69). Recall another Sabbath when this horn was exalted. God poured fresh oil on his anointed one, and he rose victoriously from the grave and ascended on high forever, scattering his enemies and securing our destiny—to glorify God—and our destination—the home Jesus is preparing for us.

God scattered his enemies, but he gathers his people (Jer. 29:14). I love the intimacy and comfort of this word. Scripture sometimes describes death as being gathered: "Abraham breathed his last and died in a good old age, an old man and full of years, and was gathered to his people" (Gen. 25:8; see 35:29; 49:33).

The psalmist prayed, "Save us, O LORD our God, / and gather us from among the nations, / that we may give thanks to your holy name / and glory in your praise" (Ps. 106:47).

A gospel gathering was anticipated when "the time is coming to gather all nations and tongues. And they shall come and shall see my glory. . . . And they shall declare my glory among the nations" (Isa. 66:18–19).

And on this side of the cross we anticipate the full gathering: "Now concerning the coming of our Lord Jesus Christ and our being gathered together to him, we ask you, brothers, not to be quickly shaken in mind or alarmed. . . . Stand firm. . . . Now may our Lord Jesus Christ himself, and God our Father, who loved us and gave us eternal comfort and good hope through grace, comfort your hearts and establish them in every good work and word" (2 Thess. 2:1–2, 15–17).

But how do we stand firm? How will we be comforted and established *now*? Jesus said: "O Jerusalem, Jerusalem [O church]. . . . How often would I have gathered your children together as a hen gathers her brood under her wings, and you were not willing!" (Matt. 23:37). Jerusalem was not willing, but are we? Jesus uses the tender imagery of a mother gathering her brood. Just as he did with Peter, Jesus calls us: "Come to me, all who labor and are heavy laden, and I will give you rest" (Matt. 11:28). It really is that stunningly simple. Are we willing to repent and turn to Jesus? We never outgrow our need for the grace of repentance.

Growing in Grace

Repenting women who find rest in Jesus become life-giving women who flourish as gatherers. When our heart is Christ's home, we can become homey places for troubled hearts to find refuge, even if we are confined to a hospital bed. Pray for grace to cultivate a welcoming place for the discouraged and lonely. Aging with grace increases our capacity for this gathering ministry.

Stay Close

Psalm 92 is a communal hymn. Those planted in the house of the Lord sang it together. The Greek word for church, *ekklesia*, generally means "the earthly gathering of God's elect."[5] Flourishing happens in community. Old age is a time to press in close to community life. Even if we cannot always attend, we can pray for and encourage others.

It takes spiritual discipline to look up and maintain an eternal perspective. We need the means of grace—Scripture, prayer, worship, sacraments—to remind us. We need fellowship with God's people to inspire us. Paul reminds us of the contrast between the destiny and destination of those who hope in God and those who do not. He encourages us to stay close to the gathered ones.

> Keep your eyes on those who walk according to the example you have in us. For many . . . walk as enemies of the cross of Christ. Their end is destruction . . . and they glory in their shame, with minds set on earthly things. But our citizenship is in heaven, and from it we await a Savior, the Lord Jesus Christ, who will transform our lowly body to be like his glorious body, by the power that enables him even to subject all things to himself. (Phil. 3:17–21)

When we gather with others in our local church, we look around and see hopeful exiles who are awaiting the Savior. We see women whose husbands left them, parents grieving the death of a child, widows and widowers, a young mom who is battling cancer, the elderly who live with chronic pain but a constant smile. The pain and sorrow of this world spills into their lives,

5   Philip Graham Ryken, *The Communion of Saints: Living in Fellowship with the People of God* (Phillipsburg, NJ: P&R, 2001), 4.

but these earthly realities do not stifle their growth in grace. They grieve, but not as those without hope (1 Thess. 4:13).

Dear reader-friend, by the power of the resurrected Christ, be one of the hopeful ones who make the moment-by-moment choice to trust and obey Jesus. Then you will give a flourishing legacy to the next generation. They can look to you and say, "I know she's lonely since her husband died," or "I know she's sad her children do not trust Jesus," or "I know it's hard being dependent on a caregiver," but look at her . . .

[She does] not lose heart. Though [her] outer nature is wasting away, [her] inner nature is being renewed day by day. For this light momentary affliction is preparing for [her] an eternal weight of glory beyond all comparison, as [she looks] not to the things that are seen but to the things that are unseen. For the things that are seen are transient, but the things that are unseen are eternal. (2 Cor. 4:16–18)

Growing in Grace

Jesus reminds us of the importance of covenant community when he says, "Where two or three are gathered in my name, there am I among them" (Matt. 18:20). A temptation of old age is to withdraw, but we flourish when we gather with God's people, because he is there.

When our grandchildren Hunter and Mary Kate were four and six years old, we drove through a beautiful neighborhood to see the elaborate Christmas lights. As we passed lavish homes, one and then the other said with wonder, "Our mansion is bigger than that one." I wondered if they really thought their modest home was a mansion, so I asked, "What mansion are you talking about?" One of them responded, "Our mansion in heaven." Three years later their baby sister, Annie Grace, died. A couple of weeks after her death, we celebrated Mary Kate's birthday. When she opened her present from her younger sister Suzie, she said, "I want this to be from Suzie *and* Annie because I know Annie has a gift for me made from gold and jewels that she will give me one day." That, my sisters, is the ultimate reality—not because Annie deserves to be in heaven, nor because we deserve to join her there, but because of God's amazing grace Annie fulfilled her destiny and went to her destination.

Pam's Story

Pam Benton lives in Nashville, Tennessee. She and her husband have three children and ten grandchildren. Pam has mentored countless seminary wives and loves teaching women God's word.

At age seventy, I did not feel old. I thought life would continue as it had for Wilson and me for the last fifty years. After Wilson retired from the pastorate, we accepted a call to another church. Something about Wilson's preaching alerted me things were different. For forty-five years Wilson preached without notes, but he started forgetting little things. The doctor diagnosed him with mild cognitive impairment. Our plans for the next fifteen years disappeared. Wilson and I both longed to "flourish like a green leaf" (Prov.11:28) as long as God gave us breath, but what would flourishing look like now?

That was seven years ago. One of the biggest challenges I continue to face is *what I want* in my life now and *what is*. Daily I ask myself, Do you believe his plans for us are "plans for welfare and not for evil, to give you a future and a hope" (Jer. 29:11)?

Just when I feel useless because I am not "the pastor's wife" and I'm not sure of my role, the Lord encourages me that loving and helping his people flourish is his call for me in this season. I am thankful I can still teach women's Bible studies, mentor young moms, disciple pastors' wives, and host guests in our home.

As Alzheimer's is stealing my husband's memory and his needs grow greater and my strength weakens, the body of Christ grows more precious. Friends take him to Bible study, hiking, and out to lunch and breakfast, and they are available to help me. As they come alongside Wilson and me, I am enabled to help other women flourish.

But, as Wilson continues to decline, the day might come when I cannot invest in the lives of others. What will flourishing look like then? The most important way to demonstrate Jesus in me is to love, honor, and care for Wilson. It is hard and sad. I could never do it without the one who promises to give us strength. Our children remind me that this season may be the most important of all our years of ministry as others observe our "long goodbye." By God's power may I "sprout and bloom profusely" till he calls me home. Even as his memory is slipping away, Wilson reminds me daily, "'Whate'er my God ordains is right,' and it is good!"[6]

Questions for Reflection and Discussion

1. Which *Growing in Grace* principle is especially helpful to you at this point in your life and why?

2. What do you see when you gather with your church family?

3. How are you a gatherer?

---

6 From Samuel Rodigast's 1675 hymn, "Whate'er My God Ordains Is Right." To learn how the church can help, see Jamie Dean, "Not Forgotten," *World Magazine*, May 23, 2019, https://world.wng.org/2019/05/not_forgotten.

4

Matriarchs of the Exile
Jeremiah 29

SHARON

Forty-year-old Mary Winslow arrived in America in 1814 with her ten children. She dreamed of building a new life with her husband, who would soon join them from Scotland. Instead, shortly after her baby daughter died, Mary learned her husband had also died.

Depression and despondency overwhelmed Mary for many months. In time, the Lord delivered her and turned her darkness into light. Rather than resenting that dark place, she later said, "I think I have learned more of my dreadfully wicked heart, and the preciousness of Jesus during this trial than I ever learnt before."[1] Through her sorrow, she experienced treasures in the darkness (Isa. 45:2–3) that enabled her to offer encouragement to others in dark places.

Mary was forty years old when she experienced these sorrows. When I was forty-five, Chuck and I looked forward to enjoying the last two years of our son Mark's high school career and preparing him for adulthood. But within a six-month span, our son Chuck graduated from college, our son Dan started college, our daughter Heidi married, and Mark was in a fatal car accident. Suddenly Chuck and I were alone. The most mundane tasks created emotional havoc as each one reminded me, "Mark is gone." I could not bear the thought of growing old with such grief and despair. I longed for heaven.

In my search for hope, I stumbled upon *Heaven Opened: The Correspondence of Mary Winslow*, compiled by her son, Octavius. Mary died around the age of eighty. One way she flourished throughout her life was through writing letters that challenged recipients to fall more in love with Jesus and to implicitly trust him. To a newly bereaved widow she asked, "How are you traveling heavenward?"[2]

This penetrating question burned into my soul and confronted me with a choice. Would I stay a prisoner to my grief or trust God to use my grief as a path to deeper understanding of his love and purpose for my life? Walking

---

1 Octavius Winslow, ed., *Heaven Opened: The Correspondence of Mary Winslow* (Grand Rapids, MI: Reformation Heritage, 2001), foreword.

2 Winslow, *Heaven Opened*, 123.

the path God marked out for me toward heaven captured my imagination.

I didn't fully understand the theological basis for Mary's question until I studied the lives of the people listed in Hebrews 11 who walked by faith, seeing themselves as exiles on this earth who were traveling to a better place:[3]

> By faith Abraham obeyed when he was called to go out to a place that he was to receive as an inheritance. And he went out, not knowing where he was going. By faith he went to live in the land of promise. . . . For he was looking forward to the city that has foundations, whose designer and builder is God. (Heb. 11:8–10)

God comforted me when I read that these saints died without experiencing the fulfillment of all God's promises, but they trusted him to keep every promise in his time:

> These all died in faith, not having received the things promised, but having seen them and greeted them from afar, and having acknowledged that they were strangers and exiles on the earth. For people who speak thus make it clear that they are seeking a homeland. If they had been thinking of that land from which they had gone out, they would have had opportunity to return. But as it is, they desire a better country, that is, a heavenly one. Therefore God is not ashamed to be called their God, for he has prepared for them a city. (Heb. 11:13–16)

---

3   This study led to the book *Treasures of Faith: Living Boldly in View of God's Promises*, coauthored with my husband, Chuck (Phillipsburg, NJ: P&R, 1999).

My grief caused me to admit my status as an exile. Somehow acknowledging I lived in a sin-broken world helped make sense out of my sorrow. Francis Schaeffer's classic question gave me more clarity: *How should we then live?*

Enter the matriarchs of Jeremiah, who faced similar questions about their destiny and destination when the Israelites were exiled to Babylon. Dig into their story, and you'll see a startling picture of the two paths highlighted in Psalm 92. Because the Israelites repeatedly chose the path of the stupid man (Ps. 92:6), God exiled them just as he warned he would do. Desperate to go back home, they turned to false prophets who promised deliverance within two years. God instructed Jeremiah to write a letter to the Israelites in exile.

The Matriarchs' Story

⁴ Thus says the LORD of hosts, the God of Israel, to all the exiles whom I have sent into exile from Jerusalem to Babylon: ⁵ Build houses and live in them; plant gardens and eat their produce. ⁶ Take wives and have sons and daughters; take wives for your sons, and give your daughters in marriage, that they may bear sons and daughters; multiply there, and do not decrease. ⁷ But seek the welfare of the city where I have sent you into exile, and pray to the Lord on its behalf, for in its welfare you will find your welfare. . . .

¹⁰ "For thus says the LORD: When seventy years are completed for Babylon, I will visit you, and I will fulfill to you my promise and bring you back to this place. (Jer. 29:4–7, 10)

"I have sent [you] into exile" (29:4) is jarring, but look closely. God speaks to his people as Yahweh, the one who entered into a personal, covenant relationship with them. He added the term *hosts*, referring to his sovereignty over all heavenly and earthly powers. It was in this context of reminding them of his steadfast love (*hesed*) and sovereignty that God assured them their captivity was his doing. To think biblically, we must think big. We are in exile because our first parents brought sin and death into the world, but *God sent his Son into exile* to redeem us. "It was the will of the LORD to crush him" (Isa. 53:10). And Peter preached that Jesus was "delivered up according to the definite plan and foreknowledge of God" (Acts 2:23). When, like him, we say "not as I will, but as you will" (Matt. 26:39), our exile will become a redemptive story. So God gives specific instructions for exile-living.

The people were to settle down and flourish (Jer. 29:5–7). They were to fulfill their destiny and glorify God in a foreign land. They likely thought temporary housing would be sufficient—until God exploded that idea. It would be seventy years (29:10).

Imagine the shock and disappointment as these exiled Israelites digested Jeremiah's words. Many of them would die before God's deliverance. When I read this, my thoughts immediately went to women my age, the matriarchs of Jeremiah 29. Anyone who has experienced loss can easily imagine how these elderly women felt when they learned

God's promise of earthly deliverance was not for them. They would not see their beloved homeland again. Change is hard at any age, but the older we are, the harder change becomes, especially when forced to let go of the familiar.

And then God comforts them. He gives them hope. He points them, and us, to Jesus. As you read these verses note God's sovereign initiative—the things *he will do.*

COMFORT

> [11] For I know the plans I have for you, declares the LORD, plans for welfare and not for evil, to give you a future and a hope. [12] Then you will call upon me and come and pray to me, and I will hear you. [13] You will seek me and find me, when you seek me with all your heart. [14] I will be found by you, declares the LORD, and I will restore your fortunes and gather you from all the nations and all the places where I have driven you, declares the LORD, and I will bring you back to the place from which I sent you into exile. (Jer. 29:11–14)

The exiles had at least three options, the same choices that face us. Of course the consequences of their choices were the same for men and women, but we will specifically think about what the options meant for the women.

Option 1. Refuse to repent of idolatry, escape from Babylon, and go to Egypt, a place of godlessness.

Jeremiah 44 is a story of defiance, doom, and destruction. God repeatedly calls out some of the Israelite women who are now in exile in Egypt for their part in preparing food for idols and in essence leading the worship of a goddess of sexual perversion (see Jer. 7:18; 44:9–24).

These women claimed that their worship of the perverse queen of heaven, Asheroth, brought blessings and that obedience to Yahweh brought loss. Jeremiah warns their actions will bring death not only to them but to their children. Rather than flourish, their temporary blessings would soon die like the grass (Ps. 92:7). Could there be any clearer picture of life-taking women?

Option 2: Stay in Babylon but do not trust the promise. Grow bitter and rebellious toward God.

These women stayed with the Israelite community in Babylon, but their anger toward God for taking them into exile tinged any obedience to his instructions with discouragement and purposelessness. Perhaps they joined in the efforts to build homes and plant gardens, but on the inside bitter roots multiplied and defiled many (Heb. 12:15). They were life-takers. I imagine some of them decided they were too old to change, too old to die to self and adapt to a new situation. Women today whose lives are turned upside down by circumstances beyond their control and who respond with ongoing bitterness and discontent wreak havoc on the very ones they love. They lose sight of God doing something bigger and better than they can imagine.

Option 3: Trust God's plan, repent of their idolatry, and in humility allow suffering to cleanse their hearts. Obey God and glorify him in Babylon for the sake of the next generation.

Making this choice meant trusting God and surrendering to his plan. It meant believing their personal freedom and happiness were not as important as leaving a legacy of faith to the next generation.

The ravages of aging may feel like exile. We are all trapped in bodies that break down over time. Regrets stir up hunger to live our lives over again. Beloved people leave our lives, whether through broken relationships or death. We worry our money will run out, and ask who will take care of us when we can't care for ourselves. We feel helpless as precious grandchildren or spiritual children make life choices we know will lead to chaos and heartache. Scripture promises we can flourish and be fruitful, but our throwaway culture tempts us to believe we are dispensable. We begin to believe our value is in what we do, rather than in whose we are.

How do we travel heavenward? How then shall we live in this foreign land of aging? Can God's instructions to the exiled Israelites guide us? Can they help us flourish? Can seeing some of his promises from "afar off" be enough to live and die by faith? Let's take a closer look at God's instructions.

The Matriarchs and Us

> [5] Build houses . . . plant gardens. . . . [6] Take wives [and husbands] and have sons and daughters . . . ; multiply there, and do not decrease. (Jer. 29:5–6)

God's first instructions to the Israelites in their captivity center on the physical home. After a five-hundred-mile march, their captors most likely settled them in a region devastated by war between Babylonia and Assyria. Settling down, building houses, and planting gardens meant cleaning up rubble, moving boulders, building homes for each family, and toiling in garden planting. They were to restore this wasted land into a viable community. The cultural mandate given to Adam and Eve to "be fruitful and multiply . . . and have dominion" was and still is in effect, even as exiles (Gen. 1:28). We are to flourish wherever we are by claiming that place for God's glory.

Israelite culture respected, honored, and cared for the older generation and in particular, older women. Though the elderly women might not be able to physically build houses, their status in the family gave them a key opportunity to influence the attitudes and stability of their households. They could be life-givers or life-takers. They could choose to joyfully embrace God's call to cultivate a godly, peaceful community or they could choose bitterness, whining, and complaining, and so can we.

Peter, in his hopeful letter to elect exiles, gives strikingly similar instructions to the women.

> Wives, be subject to your own husbands, so that even if some do not obey the word, they may be won without a word by the conduct of their wives, when they see your respectful and pure conduct. . . . Let your adorning be the hidden person of the heart with the imperishable beauty of a gentle and quiet spirit, which in God's sight is very

precious. For this is how the *holy women* who *hoped in God* used to adorn themselves. . . .

Husbands . . . [show] honor to the woman . . . since they are *heirs with you of the grace of life.* (1 Pet. 3:1–7)

Peter coupled his instructions with a reminder of women who went before them—women who were holy and hopeful heirs of the grace of life. This reminded me that as a recipient of God's mercy, I, too, had a key place of influence in our home after Mark's death. The rubble of grief in our home seemed impossible to clear so that joy and peace could find a place. But Paul's words in Ephesians 2:10 reassured me that God had already equipped me for my destiny: "For we are his workmanship, created in Christ Jesus for good works, which God prepared beforehand, that we should walk in them."

I could not and did not need to walk this journey alone. Walking by faith in the abyss of grief could not be done in isolation, no matter how tempted I was to hide in my sorrow. Like the matriarchs of Jeremiah, God's call to trust him presented me with choices every minute of every day. Would I embrace my destiny and invite others to "taste and see that the LORD is good" (Ps. 34:8), or would I nurse my wounds and adopt a victim mentality? Would I choose to soak in his word, worship privately and corporately, pray fervently, and allow others to walk with me? Or would I resign myself to a life of emotional and spiritual hard labor, with no expectation of joy and peace this side of heaven? Could I minute by minute die to self, trusting the Lord to grow the fruit others needed for their spiritual growth?

In chapter 3 Susan reminds us that it takes spiritual discipline to look up and maintain an eternal perspective. We need the means of grace—Scripture, prayer, worship, sacraments—to remind us. We need fellowship with God's people to inspire us. Paul reminds us of the contrast between the destiny and destination of those who hope in God and those who do not. He encourages us to stay close to the hopeful ones: "Keep your eyes on those who walk according to the example you have in us" (Phil. 3:17).

I made a choice to stay close to the "hopeful ones" who spoke scriptural truth into my life, not just with words but also with their actions. Our daughter Heidi's wedding was six months after Mark's accident. I couldn't think clearly; my chest ached. Planning a wedding felt impossible. The modern matriarchs, my dear friends, saw the rubble of my life but linked arms to not only help us give our daughter in marriage, but to prepare our home for this joyous occasion. One friend showed up every week, sometimes with cleaning supplies, other times with paint chips. She organized teams to clean and paint. Other friends gathered to decorate the church, and to encourage our daughter to enjoy this sweet season of her life. These friends were "hopeful ones" whose love for Jesus compelled them to walk in the darkness with our family.

⁷ Seek the welfare of the city where I have sent you. (Jer. 29:7)

The Israelites' behavior toward their neighbors would demonstrate God's love. Again, Peter gives similar instructions in his letter to elect exiles.

> You are a chosen race, a royal priesthood, a holy nation, a people for his own possession, that you may proclaim the excellencies of him who called you out of darkness into his marvelous light. . . .
>
> Beloved, I urge you as sojourners and exiles to abstain from the passions of the flesh, which wage war against your soul. Keep your conduct among the Gentiles honorable, so that when they speak against you as evildoers, they may see your good deeds and glorify God on the day of visitation. (1 Pet. 2:9–12)

Like the Israelite women and the women Peter wrote to who were scattered throughout what is modern-day Turkey, like the woman who recently moved to live with her son or daughter or to a retirement home, and like countless women in other new and unexpected places, I needed hope, a destiny that made life worth living. What can enable us to live in a way that can help turn the hearts of the next generation toward God? God's love flows from his next words.

> ¹¹ For I know the plans I have for you, declares the LORD, plans for welfare and not for evil, to give you a future and a hope. (Jer. 29:11)

Tikvah is the word we translate as "hope." The Hebrews knew the deeper meaning of this beautiful word. *Tikvah* is the word translated as "cord" in Joshua 2:18, 21. Rahab's hope for rescue rested in a scarlet cord.

In Ezekiel God's people cried out, "Our hope [*tikvah*] is lost; we are indeed cut off" Ezek. 37:11). But they were wrong. God showed his trustworthiness and power to bring life from what appeared to be dead by breathing life into a valley of dry bones and creating a vast army (see Ezek. 37:1–14). Where there appeared to be no hope, there was unbroken hope.

The prophet Isaiah declares life will come out of what appears to be a dead stump: "There shall come forth a shoot from the stump [*tikvah*] of Jesse, / and a branch from his roots shall bear fruit" (Isa. 11:1). In that dead stump is unbroken hope. Jesus is the shoot, coming in glory when all seems hopeless.

You may be surrounded by rubble, just as the Israelites were. How do God's instructions to them apply to us? Remember, living as an exile committed to glorifying God is a process, not an event.

Our destiny is to glorify God and our destination is heaven. At one point after Mark's death, Chuck said, "Mark's death unbolted me from my love affair with this world." Later, I shared his words with a bereaved mother. She responded, "When I heard Chuck's words, I could hear the chains dropping." Seeing ourselves as elect exiles, looking forward to a better place prepared for us in heaven by our Savior, unshackles us to see each circumstance as an opportunity to know God better and trust him more—to flourish.

Throughout their capture and subsequent captivity, it's likely the Israelites feared God had forsaken them. Maybe they thought they deserved abandonment because of their great sin. Instead, our loving Father reassured them that though he sent them into captivity because of their sin, his intentions toward them were forgiveness, mercy, love. He is not an absent Father. Though they may not have felt his presence, he could not break his promise to never leave them, no matter how painful their pathway. Where they were at the moment was not all there was. God had an expected end in mind that would surely come to pass.

Likewise, when the path on which God has placed us seems impossible and we cry out that our hope is lost, the Lord reminds us to cling to the cord of hope that cannot be broken. When all seems lost, God keeps his promises and breathes life into what appears to be dead. When life crumbles around us and we wonder if God has lost control, we see Jesus (Heb. 2:9), the fulfillment of God's greatest promise. Our expected end, the one to which Christians cling, is the fulfillment of all of God's promises, culminating in being gathered to the place Jesus is preparing for us—heaven and, ultimately, the new heavens and new earth.

The bomb of grief after Mark's death left a trail of rubble and devastation. Rebuilding seemed impossible. I wrestled to reconcile God's love with his sovereignty, and at one point cried to Chuck, "If we didn't have children, I think I would walk away from my faith. Trusting God feels so much harder than blaming him." Chuck asked, "If your faith isn't good enough for you, why do you want our children to cling to the Lord?" I answered, "Because I know there is nowhere else to go for hope and help. I have to believe that at some point his grace will be enough." At one point I wanted to stop writing *Treasures in Darkness: A Grieving Mother Shares Her Heart* because going back into my journals was too painful.[4] Chuck told me, "Write for our children and grandchildren. Some day they will face horrific grief and loss. Leave a trail of hope through our story."

So dear sister, how are you traveling heavenward? Will you hope in his plan, promise, and power, or will you hope in yourself? I encourage you to join the company of holy, hopeful heirs of the grace of life. And I pray that "the God of hope [will] fill you with all joy and peace in believing, so that by the power of the Holy Spirit you may abound in hope" (Rom. 15:13).

Barbara's Story

Barbara Thompson is a retired social worker. After forty years in Zachary, Louisiana, she and her husband, Mark, along with her parents, moved to Jackson, Mississippi, near their son's family.

---

4 Sharon Betters, *Treasures in Darkness: A Grieving Mother Shares Her Heart* (Phillipsburg, NJ: P&R, 2005).

As a social worker I encountered Christians in nursing homes who flourished. Their identity as those who were "bought with a price" (1 Cor. 6:20) was evident in the fruit of the Spirit in their lives. They humbly and gratefully received care, prayed and sang with their pastors, and rejoiced and mourned with others.

Now, I am an aging caregiver, a seventy-two-year-old caring for my parents in their nineties. Caregiving is a curious label, indicating tending and nurturing beyond mothering. It is a contrast to what we Christian baby boomers expected—to retire, mature spiritually, serve with wisdom, and enjoy the benefits of our labor. I thought I would be an advocate for my parents, anticipating that their daily needs would be met by staff members. The reality of caregiving is much more granular—transport chairs, meals, errands, repetitive conversations, laundry, medications, and the relentless undertow of presence. Caregiving is not easily delegated, and any extended absence is anxiety-provoking and challenging.

I am a caregiver praying for grace to flourish in my weakness. God is inexorably challenging my competencies, selfishness, plans, and desires. As I recently trained small group leaders for our Bible study, I prayed, "Lord, this is what I love and know how to do. Isn't this how you equipped me to serve? Can't someone else care for my parents?" You know the answer! This is not what I planned, but my Father who is sovereign, faithful, good, and merciful is finishing what he has begun in me.

Glorifying God in my calling as a caregiver drives me to acknowledge my need. I desperately need the Spirit to call me to repent of caregiving out of obligation and to give myself to loving and life-giving care for my parents. I need my sisters in Christ to encourage me to think biblically and live cove-nantally. I feel as if I am taking a final exam in biblical wom-anhood. I rejoice and need reminders that my exam grade was "bought with a price" by my Savior and that God's grace, like manna, is daily. Or, as Charles Bridges wrote, "Daily progress in the heavenly walk is not maintained by yesterday's grace. Humble and dependent prayer must fetch in a fresh supply continually."[5]

Questions for Reflection and Discussion

1. Read Hebrews 11:8–16. What gave hope to Abraham and the Old Testament saints?

2. Read Philippians 3:17–20. What gives believers today hope?

3. What is your response to Mary Winslow's question "How are you traveling heavenward?"

---

5   Charles Bridges, *Psalm 119: An Exposition* (1827; repr., Carlisle, PA: Banner of Truth Trust, 1974), 21.

5

Flourishing and Fruitful
Psalm 92:12–15

SUSAN

Flourishing and fruitfulness are delightful themes of Scripture. God commanded the earth to sprout vegetation. The living creatures were commanded to "be fruitful and multiply" (see Gen. 1:11–25). The man and woman were given a cultural mandate to be fruitful and multiply *and* to have dominion over the creation. They were to live face-to-face with God and extend his glory to all the earth, foreshadowing the gospel mandate to go into all the world and be fruitful and multiply spiritually as we make disciples (Matt. 28:18–20). And in the new Jerusalem there will be the "tree of life, with its twelve kinds of fruit, yielding its fruit each month" (Rev. 22:2).

When I was young, if someone had asked me what words came to mind when I thought about aging, I suspect I would have said *declining, unproductive, dependent, inactive*. I wonder if God's declaration that his righteous ones will flourish, grow, and be fruitful in old age is on the short list of the most unexpected surprises in Scripture.

Psalm 92:12–15

¹² The righteous flourish like the palm tree
    and grow like a cedar in Lebanon.
¹³ They are planted in the house of the LORD;
    they flourish in the courts of our God.
¹⁴ They still bear fruit in old age;
    they are ever full of sap and green,
¹⁵ to declare that the LORD is upright;
    he is my rock, and there is no unrighteousness
       in him.

These verses answer the following questions:

Who does the Bible say will flourish and be fruitful?

What does the Bible mean by *flourishing* and *fruitful*?

Where is the place we learn to flourish and be fruitful?

Who Will Flourish and Be Fruitful?

The "righteous" refers to the status of God's chosen children whom he declares righteous by crediting the perfect righteousness of Christ to their account. They are the justified ones. The Westminster Shorter Catechism explains:

Justification is an act of God's free grace, wherein he pardoneth all our sins, and accepteth us as righteous in his sight, only for the righteousness of Christ imputed to us, and received by faith alone.[1]

The purpose of this book is not to share clever strategies that will equip you to become a better, older version of yourself. Instead, it's about what *God* is committed to do in the lives of his justified ones—women just like you. It's about the reversals he accomplishes by his grace.

And all the trees of the field shall know that I am the LORD;
I bring low the high tree, and make high the low tree, dry up the green tree, and make the dry tree *flourish*. I am the LORD; I have spoken, and I will do it. (Ezek. 17:24)

Growing in Grace

Our justification is an act of God's free grace. The physical and mental decline of aging does not decrease the power of his grace to reverse the effects of the fall and to make us flourish spiritually. God has spoken, and he will do it.

What Do Flourishing and Fruitful Mean?

Jesus said, "The hour has come for the Son of Man to be glorified. Truly, truly, I say to you, unless a grain of wheat falls

1 Westminster Shorter Catechism, question 33 (Lawrenceville, GA: Presbyterian Church in American Committee on Discipleship Ministries, 1990), 12.

into the earth and dies, it remains alone; but if it dies, it bears much fruit" (John 12:23–24).

R. C. Sproul's explanation of this profound passage takes us to the heart of a biblical understanding of flourishing.

Jesus spoke in the same breath of the hour of his glorification and of the hour of his death. . . . Jesus did not say that if a grain of wheat falls into the ground it *might* produce some fruit. Instead, He said that it *would* produce "much fruit." It is not possible, not even theoretically possible, that the atonement of Jesus could not bear fruit. The Father makes certain that the grain of wheat that dies bears fruit.

If you are in Christ and have tasted of the bread of heaven, you are that fruit. Indeed, the fruit encompasses the whole of Jesus' church. . . . Here we see the paradox of the Christian life that Jesus spoke about so often— we find life in dying to self and following Christ.[2]

We do not see the mysterious work of germination while the seed is in the ground, but as it is watered and warmed, it eventually sprouts, grows, blossoms, and bears fruit. This fruit does not depend on human achievement; it is other-worldly, spiritual, abundant, eternal. This is the fruit of repentance, the fruit of righteousness, the fruit of the Spirit. The world equates flourishing with activity and productivity. A biblical perspective does not mean we *do more*; it means *we become*

2   R. C. Sproul, *John,* St. Andrew's Expositional Commentary (Orlando, FL: Reformation Trust, 2009), 229–30.

more like Christ. We mature in faith, hope, and love. God himself describes this amazing process. Note what he says *he will* do.

> I will give you a new heart, and a new spirit I will put within you. And I will remove the heart of stone from your flesh and give you a heart of flesh. . . . And you shall be my people, and I will be your God. . . . I will make the fruit of the tree and the increase of the field abundant. . . . Then the nations that are left all around you shall know that I am the LORD; I have rebuilt the ruined places and replanted that which was desolate. I am the LORD; I have spoken, and I will do it. (Ezek. 36:26–30, 36)

As counterintuitive as it sounds, flourishing is a slow and progressive death that brings abundant life. Our new heart has new desires. Even as our physical bodies grow old, God causes our new desires to flourish as they are fertilized by his word and Spirit, and we die to self-centered desires, dreams, and demands. This is possible because of God's covenant promise that he will be our God, we will be his people, and he will live among us.

The specific trees mentioned in Psalm 92 show the potential of the righteous to flourish and be fruitful.

The date palm, which was common in Israel, grows straight. It is upright, majestic in its simplicity. And the older this tree becomes, the sweeter and more abundant the fruit it produces.

These tall evergreens can grow up to 30 meters tall, with large, fronded leaves which can span 4–5 meters and are tipped with sharp points. . . . In the spring, their large branches contain a multitude of small blossoms. . . . Dates are harvested in the dying days of the summer. The date palm is extremely economical, with every part of the tree having its own use.

The leaves are used to make ropes, baskets and other woven goods such as crates.

The wood is used for household interiors, furniture and exterior areas.

The leaf bases and fruit stalks can be used as fuel.

The fruit can be used for date vinegar, date chutney, sweet pickle, date paste and flavoring.[3]

Just as every part of the Judean palm has a purpose, so too nothing in our lives is wasted. God uses everything to conform us to the likeness of Jesus (Rom. 8:28–29) *and* to benefit others. Joseph's betrayal by his brothers was intended to harm him, "but God meant it for good, to bring it about that many people should be kept alive" (Gen. 50:20). Paul's imprisonment was not wasted—"I want you to know, brothers, that what has happened to me has really served to advance the gospel" (Phil. 1:12).

3 "Filming in Israel the Original Biblical Palm Trees," Biblical Productions, https://www.biblicalproductions.com/filming-in-israel/filming-in-israel-the-original-biblical-palm-trees/.

We flourish when we trust God and see that everything that happens to us is designed by him to advance the gospel in our hearts and in the hearts of others.

The magnificent cedar of Lebanon grows in the mountains. It endures the cold temperatures and strong winds and can reach one hundred feet in height with branches that spread fifty feet or more. Some are three thousand years old. Like the palm tree, they are always green. They usually grow in groves with their branches intertwining, providing a canopy of shade.

Growing in Grace

Even when our bodies become bent with age, the spirit of the Christian who dies to self and follows Christ grows upright. Like the date palm, she becomes sweeter in old age. And like the full-grown cedar of Lebanon, her presence provides a canopy of gospel refreshment for others.

Where Do We Learn to Flourish and Be Fruitful?

We flourish in the house of the Lord. Have you ever really pondered what it means to be planted in the house of the Lord? It will leave you awestruck.

> The eternal God is your dwelling place,
>   and underneath are the everlasting arms. (Deut.
>   33:27)

Lord, you have been our dwelling place
    in all generations.
Before the mountains were brought forth,
      or ever you had formed the earth and the world,
      from everlasting to everlasting you are God.
        (Ps. 90:1–2)

The Lord's redeemed ones live in his presence. We are never homeless; *he* is our home.

Paul develops this when he writes, "To the church of the Thessalonians *in God* the Father and the Lord Jesus Christ" (1 Thess. 1:1). John Stott explains that "the relationship in mind is a vital, organic union which makes possible the sharing of a common life. . . . Perhaps, then, we should paraphrase the preposition 'in' as meaning 'living in', 'rooted in' or 'drawing its life from.'" Stott continues to explain that in other places Paul refers to the *church in a particular place*, for example, in Corinth (1 Cor. 1:2), when "the preposition 'in' has a different nuance . . . since the church is 'in' God as the source from which its life comes, whereas it is 'in' the world only as the sphere in which it lives. Nevertheless, it is still correct to say that every church has two homes, two environments, two habitats. It lives in God and it lives in the world."[4] One way we live out this transcendent truth is to live in community with others who are nestled in God's heart—our local church.

---

4 John Stott, *The Gospel & the End of Time: The Message of 1 & 2 Thessalonians* (Downers Grove, IL: InterVarsity Press, 1991), 28.

A seed, or a tree, cannot plant itself. God sovereignly places us in the plot of dirt—the place on the planet and the time in history—where he intends for us to flourish. Those who are declared righteous by grace are strategically planted in God's family—the church—and nurtured by his word and Spirit so they gradually become righteous in character and conduct.

The older I get, the more I am wonderstruck at the very idea of the church, the body of Christ, the bride of Christ, the family of God. The church is the people of God in all times and places, those chosen in Christ in eternity past and who are being redeemed, justified, adopted, and sanctified in him. The church is all those who live in his presence. The church is a covenant community of those who are indwelt by God's Holy Spirit so they have the power to make Jesus known. The church is the people who have been entrusted with the living word of the living God. Praise the blessed triune God that I am a living stone in this living temple—and so are you if you trust him alone for your salvation.

The righteous woman loves the church universal and the church triumphant, and she loves the local church where God plants her at any given time. Sometimes a church is hard to love. The question is not, Is your church perfect? but rather, What is your perspective of your church? Do you love her because Jesus loves her? Do you serve her because she is the body of Christ?

As we age, the way we serve our church is usually different from the way we served in younger years. When our roles and responsibilities change, will we be resentful of younger women who replace us? Will we criticize changes they make? Or will we be sap (the blood of a tree) that carries nutrients and energy to these buds as they are forming? Will we recognize that less mobility and energy actually frees us to spend more time praying? Will we rest in the assurance that we may not see the fruit of our prayers but God will answer them in his time and his way?

Shortly after the Soviet Union collapsed in 1991, some Eastern Bloc countries allowed missionaries in. An American pastor attended a church service in Ukraine and wrote the following in his church newsletter:

> How mistaken the Communists were when they allowed the older women to continue worshipping together! It was they who were considered no threat to the new order, but it was they whose prayers and faithfulness over all those barren years held the church together and raised up a generation of men and young people to serve the Lord. Yes, the church we attended was crowded with these older women at the very front, for they had been the stalwart defenders and maintainers of Christ's Gospel, but behind them and alongside them and in the balcony and outside the windows were the fruit of their faithfulness, men, women, young people, and children. We must never underestimate the place

and power of our godly women. To them go the laurels in the Church in Ukraine![5]

By contrast, another pastor wrote a series of articles on dangerous cliques in the Western church such as the Good Ol' Boy Club and the Charter-Member Club. The one that caught my attention was the DOLC—the Domineering Old Ladies Club. These excerpts from his article on the DOLC are sobering.

> This clique . . . is made up of older women who like to think of themselves as the matriarchs of the church. . . . However, they lack any real submissiveness towards those in leadership. If you notice, they get their way and will do what it takes to bring it about. . . . Men tend to fear this group. . . . The DOLC . . . make sure that the younger women are not involved in any aspect of the women's ministries, or other ministries for that matter, when it might challenge the DOLCs control and power.[6]

Before you start naming the names of women you think match this description, let me share my friend's humble response to this article: "Busted! Lord, deliver me from being in the DOLC, and from the club that criticizes them. Lord, have mercy."

5   Glen Knecht, First Presbyterian Church, Columbia, SC, newsletter.
6   Timothy J. Hammons, "Domineering Old Ladies Club," *Thoughts That Matter* (blog), accessed 2015.

I don't know either of these pastors, but I know both groups of women because they both live in my heart, and when I let the DOLC loose, it is always destructive to others and to me.

Growing in Grace

As life slows down, we can become controlling and critical, or we can reflect on God's sovereign love that chose and planted us in his house. The more we live in the light of the reality of his presence, the more we flourish as his Spirit fills us with sap to nurture and encourage others to flourish.

Flourishing and Fruitful

God gave the first man and woman a cultural mandate to "be fruitful and multiply" (Gen. 1:28). God's equal but different image bearers had a monumental mission to fill the world with other image bearers who would reflect the glory of the Creator; instead, they listened to the destroyer. But God did not destroy them. He promised an offspring of the woman who would defeat the destroyer (Gen. 3:15). In response to this promise of life, Adam "called his wife's name Eve, because she was the mother of all living" (Gen. 3:20). *Eve* sounds like the Hebrew word for life-giver. Because of her sin, the woman became a life-taker. Because of the gospel of grace, she was declared to be a life-giver.

God's redeemed daughters have the potential to be fruitful life-givers, not just biologically but spiritually, because the life of Christ is in us. Becoming a life-giver in our relationships and circumstances is a process of dying to self, so we decrease and Jesus increases and his life flows from us to bless others. This process does not get easier as we age. The temptations may change, but our need for repentance remains the same. When we nurse our disappointments and make children and grandchildren feel guilty for not visiting more, or brood over unmet expectations, or hold grudges for decades, roots of bitterness and unforgiveness grow and we become life-takers: "See to it that no one fails to obtain the grace of God; that no 'root of bitterness' springs up and causes trouble, and by it many become defiled" (Heb. 12:15).

Perhaps you have heard an older woman say, "I've earned the right to say what I want to say," and what follows usually hurts those around her. Hear what James has to say:

> Where jealousy and selfish ambition exist, there will be disorder and every vile practice. But the wisdom from above is first pure, then peaceable, gentle, open to reason, full of mercy and good fruits, impartial and sincere. And a harvest of righteousness is sown in peace by those who make peace. (James 3:16–18)

The words *flourishing* and *fruitful* are very similar. The Hebrew word for *flourishing* is *parach*, which means to bud, sprout, or blossom. The word for *fruitful* is *parch*, which means bearing fruit, flourishing, or increasing. The combination gives a rich and clear picture of God's plan for his righteous ones in every season and circumstance of life. The word *life-giver* pulsates with the idea of flourishing and fruitful.

Growing in Grace

Life-takers leave a legacy that defiles many. Life-givers leave a legacy that blesses many as they bear "fruit in keeping with repentance" (Matt. 3:8) and the fruit of the Spirit: "love, joy, peace, patience, kindness, goodness, faithfulness, gentleness, self-control" (Gal. 5:22–23).

This gospel wonder is possible because of God's grace. A righteous woman can therefore declare the following with her heart and lips.

"The Lord is upright" (Ps. 92:15). This speaks of God's character, which assures us he will always do right. He will be true to every promise. He is perfect in his faithfulness. There is credibility in an older woman's declaration that he never left her, even in her darkest places and times.

"He is my Rock." Hannah declared. "There is none holy like the Lord: / for there is none besides you; / there is no rock like our God" (1 Sam. 2:2). The house built on the rock is not destroyed by floods and winds (Matt. 7:24–25). There is something profoundly persuasive about a woman weak and withered by age singing:

My hope is built on nothing less than Jesus' blood and
    righteousness;
I dare not trust the sweetest frame, but wholly lean on
    Jesus' name.
On Christ, the solid rock, I stand;
All other ground is sinking sand, all other ground is
    sinking sand.[7]

"There is no unrighteousness in him." If there was even a
hint of unrighteousness in Christ, he could not be our righteousness. This is a declaration of confidence—not self-
confidence but *Christ*-confidence. We declare that he is our
dwelling place and we are clothed in the perfect righteousness
of Christ.

When my husband was a church planter, our church met
for several years in a store building. There were no older people in our congregation until Mrs. Johnston came. This radiant woman loved Jesus, and she loved us. When she moved to
an assisted-living facility and was not able to attend church, I
cherished my visits with this life-giving spiritual mother. One
day she told me about the television preachers she enjoyed
watching. Then she surprised me when she said, "But I never
watch them on Sunday morning because when our church is
worshiping, I join you and pray for all of you." Mrs. Johnston
knew the transcendent wonder of the church triumphant and
the nearness of being a part of a local covenant community,

7 Edward Mote, "My Hope Is Built on Nothing Less," 1834.

and she joined her heart to ours in the joy of worship. Sometimes I took my Sunday school class to visit her. The children loved singing and reciting Bible verses for her, and she loved them big from her hospital bed in a small room. One Sunday our lesson was on joy. I asked the children, "What is joy?" Without hesitating one of the boys said, "Mrs. Johnston." No one laughed; they all agreed. They had seen the joy that radiates from a worshiping heart.

Mrs. Johnston lived in God's presence—in relationship with him. Her life and lips declared the power and beauty of his grace. She thought, prayed, and loved biblically. She grew in the grace and knowledge of Jesus until the end, which was really the beginning.

Jerdone's Story

Jerdone Davis, of Seneca, South Carolina, retired consecutively from working as a registered nurse, mentoring college women in the college ministry Reformed University Fellowship, and teaching as professor of Christian education at Erskine Theological Seminary. Currently semiretired, she teaches nurses and other medical personnel while volunteering at her church as a Bible teacher and as a faith community nurse.[8]

Flourishing reminds me of my recent success with a gift, a Christmas cactus shocked during its move into my home.

---

8   To learn more about faith community nursing, visit the websites for the Westberg Institute, https://westberginstitute.org/ and Health Ministries Association, https://hmassoc.org. Many states have local associations as well.

Every bud died. Placing it in the warm sunlight and infrequent watering nurtured its healthy response of multiple red blossoms.

This plant is a metaphor for my thriving in old age. As a single woman, never married, with no children, I face a future without family. Occasionally, perceiving my aloneness or contemplating old-age illnesses, even death, overwhelms my emotions. In those times of anxiety and fear, I cling to God's promise never to forsake me because I am his, and the shock dissipates into peace and joy.

Retirement was terrorizing at first, until the Lord stabilized me by his nurture and assurance, giving me treasures of continued opportunities to share his grace. God planted me in a church family that loves well. We experience life's ups and downs together, holding each other by worship, prayer, and fellowship.

At each professional crossroads, God has called me to invest his word in practical, tangible ways. As retirement loomed near, I wondered how he would use my gifts and talents. Then, with a nurse's sixth sense, I observed the signs of illness in a close friend at church, inquired, and then encouraged her to seek medical advice. She, her husband, and I held our breath as the diagnosis was given: stage 4 colon cancer. God had given me a vision to bring faith community nursing to bear in our congregation. A "care team" committee of five quickly organized to aid the church in loving this couple well, arranging meals, structured short visits, and transportation to medical appointments. Friends all over the world participated in her care by an internet service used to chronicle her journey into wellness. Today, with joy and peace we flourish physically, spiritually, and emotionally.

God promises in his word, "I will give you the treasures of darkness / and the hoards in secret places, / that you may know that it is I, the LORD, / . . . who [calls] you by your name" (Isa. 45:3). Often upon awaking, I am singing "It is well with my soul." Whether by teaching nursing and Bible for our women, or by acting as a faith community nurse, my life in retirement is full of God's promises. There is no fear, only sustaining peace and joy.

Questions for Reflection and Discussion

1. How would you explain a biblical perspective of flourishing?

2. Which *Growing in Grace* principle is especially helpful to you at this point in your life and why?

3. Reflect on the examples of the Ukrainian women and the Domineering Old Ladies Club (DOLC). How is each kind of woman a life-taker or a life-giver? What legacy does each leave in her family and church?

6

Elizabeth
Luke 1:5–48

SHARON

Maybe you're thinking, I understand the biblical principle of flourishing explained in chapter 5, but I don't see how it's possible for me to flourish when . . .

I'm estranged from my children.

I can't move past my grief.

All my friends have moved or died; I'm alone and no one cares.

I gave up on God giving me the desires of my heart a long time ago; it's too late for me.

You are not alone in feeling helpless. Growing in grace is impossible, not just for you but for all of us—yet Jesus said, "What is impossible with man is possible with God" (Luke 18:27). God promises that when we are planted in his house, he will do the impossible—grow fruit that shows up in old people, fruit designed to not only transform our fearful hearts to peaceful, trusting hearts as we navigate the foreign land of old age, but fruit that nourishes others as well. As we will see in the story of Elizabeth, sometimes we don't recognize the fruit of a life rooted in Jesus until confronted with the challenges of aging.

The motif of a barren wife being fruitful runs throughout Scripture, beginning with Sarah, who laughed at the idea of flourishing since she was past the age of childbearing. The Lord's question then is his question now, to us: "Is anything too hard for the LORD?" (Gen. 18:14).

When the angel announced the birth of Jesus, young Mary asked how it could be possible for a virgin to be fruitful and multiply. The angel answered with an explanation and an example.

Explanation: "And the angel answered her, 'The Holy Spirit will come upon you, and the power of the Most High will overshadow you; therefore the child to be born will be called holy—the Son of God'" (Luke 1:35).

Example: "And behold, your relative Elizabeth in her old age has also conceived a son, and this is the sixth month with her who was called barren. For nothing will be impossible with God" (Luke 1:36–37).

The angel explained the gospel wonder of the Holy Spirit giving life, and gave a flesh-and-blood example—Elizabeth—to show the power of the gospel to do the impossible in and through us. The gospel story written into Elizabeth's story can be true for us because the storyline is the same: when the Holy Spirit gives us a new heart, it is possible for us to flourish and be fruitful spiritually even in old age because God has spoken and he will do it (Ezek. 36:26–36).

Elizabeth's Story

> [5] In the days of Herod, king of Judea, there was a priest named Zechariah, of the division of Abijah. And he had a wife from the daughters of Aaron, and her name was Elizabeth. [6] And they were both righteous before God, walking blamelessly in all the commandments and statutes of the Lord. [7] But they had no child, because Elizabeth was barren, and both were advanced in years. (Luke 1:5–7)

Elizabeth and Zechariah lived in a time when spiritual darkness hung like a menacing cloud over God's people. It had been about four hundred years since God's people heard his voice, and many believed he had forgotten his promise. Israel turned away from God to a religion of works and self-righteousness. The political climate was chaotic under King Herod's terrifying reign. The Old Testament ends with the promise that the sun will rise when the light of the world, Messiah, comes and destroys the darkness (see Mal. 3:16–18; 4:1–3). Elizabeth and Zechariah hoped in this promise.

PLANTED IN THE HOUSE OF THE LORD

Both Elizabeth and Zechariah were descendants of Aaron, the original high priest chosen by God to represent the people before him and to butcher the lambs brought for sacrifice. Their parents' tenacious belief in God's promised Redeemer showed up in their children's names: Zechariah means "God remembers." Elizabeth means "oath of God" or "my God has sworn." Both families passed on to their children their hope in the promises of God.

Biblical hope is the rich soil of flourishing. But how do we live as we wait for hope to become reality? Elizabeth's life shows how *hope* and *waiting* intertwine. These words are often used interchangeably, depending on the English translation, as in Psalm 25:3:

> No one who *hopes* in you / will ever be put to shame. (NIV)
> Indeed, none who *wait* for you shall be put to shame. (ESV)

Hope and *wait* are often used in the same verse: "And now, O Lord, for what do I wait? / My hope is in you" (Ps. 39:7).[1]

What does waiting in hope look like in daily life?

> They who wait [hope] for the Lord shall renew their
>   strength;
>   they shall mount up with wings like eagles;
> they shall run and not be weary;
>   they shall walk and not faint. (Isa. 40:31)

1   Other hope/wait scriptures include Ps. 62:5; Rom. 8:24–25.

The root meaning for *wait* in this passage is "to bind together (perhaps by twisting)."[2]

This is not a picture of a string tied around a bundle of newspapers but rather strings that are intertwined. When a rope of many strands is used to pull a heavy load, the weight of the load stretches the strings, pulling them tighter together. The harder the job, the more tightly wound the strings become. *Wait* is an action word. Isaiah explains that waiting with hope, a sometimes exhausting journey, means twisting ourselves around the Lord and binding ourselves to him. When we cling to him, a supernatural exchange slowly but surely happens: his strength becomes our strength. The harder the waiting, the more tightly wound we are to him. Elizabeth was probably familiar with this promise; her life shows us the fruit of hopeful waiting. Instead of becoming weak spiritually as she aged, she soared like an eagle as she was increasingly satisfied with the Lord.

> Bless the LORD, O my soul,
>> and all that is within me,
>> bless his holy name! . . .
> who satisfies you with good
>> so that your youth is renewed like the eagle's. (Ps.
>> 103:1, 5)

We meet Elizabeth when she is an old woman; Luke reminds us three times she is old. She is an unlikely example of

2 James Strong, *Strong's Expanded Exhaustive Concordance of the Bible* (Nashville: Thomas Nelson, 1990), s.v. "qavah."

a woman aging with grace because she experienced a life of barrenness, yet she is called blameless. *Barren* refers to land incapable of producing vegetation. It means unproductive, infertile, unfruitful, sterile, waste, desolate. It's the opposite of flourishing. So immediately we know this is a story of the reversals accomplished by God's grace. As we ask Elizabeth *how we can flourish* even in old age, I imagine her, with twinkling eyes, calling back to us, "Listen to my story, and see how God taught me to die to self and twist myself around him by waiting in hope, even when he denied me the desire of my heart."

BLAMELESS AND BARREN

Like many devout young Jewish girls, Elizabeth probably hoped God would choose her to bear the promised Messiah. She longed to be fruitful and multiply, but experienced the grief of barrenness and the gut-wrenching pain of judgment and gossip from her neighbors who believed childlessness was a curse from God, a punishment for some sin, and most likely the woman's fault.[3] She also bore the shame of not bearing a son to carry on the family name, and the fear of not having a son to care for Zechariah and her in their old age. Did she ever cry to Zechariah, as Rachel did to Jacob, "Give me children, or I shall die!" (Gen. 30:1)?

Think of the sorrow passing between husband and wife when Elizabeth looked into Zechariah's hopeful eyes, month

3   See Gen. 16:4, 11; 29:32; 30:1; 1 Sam. 1:5–6, 11; 2:5, 7–8.

after month, and silently shook her head no. Imagine the deep grief when menopause came and they knew they would never conceive. Consider Elizabeth's private struggle to understand her identity and role when she could not bear a son. But through it all, Scripture tells us what determined their response to their pain and disappointment. Their status was "righteous before God"—he declared them justified by his grace. They flourished by "walking blamelessly in all the commandments and statutes of the Lord" (Luke 1:6). This description tells us that whether happy or brokenhearted, they confidently declared their hope in God by living according to his word. They thought biblically and they lived covenantally. We don't know the specifics of how this played out in Elizabeth's life, but consider some of the possible implications for her.

- Her marriage flourished. She died to her expectations and learned to comfort and encourage her husband rather than withdraw into her own pain. This strand of three cords became stronger (Eccles. 4:12).
- She remained involved in covenant community life, even though it continually confronted her with families who were multiplying. When a baby was born into their church family, she died to her disappointment and rejoiced in this covenant child. She even helped young mothers and encouraged them to teach their children to walk in the ways of the Lord.
- When other women were unkind about her barrenness, she prayed that God would not let a bitter root

grow in her heart and defile others (Heb. 12:15). When bitterness did take root, she repented of her sin and asked God to cleanse her heart.

- Perhaps she repeatedly fed her mind and heart with Habakkuk 3:17–18: "Though the fig tree should not blossom, /nor fruit be on the vines, / . . . yet I will rejoice in the LORD; / I will take joy in the God of my salvation."

- Her perspective of her life and of the world was God-centered and not self-centered.

- In contrast to many Jews who lived for man's approval, she worshiped God and through bloody sacrifices demonstrated her need for a Savior. As hope for a child died, the greater hope of the promised Messiah flourished and made her sweeter in old age. Her theology shaped her daily life.

Long before the Lord gave Elizabeth her miracle baby, her life illustrated God's promise to make the dry tree flourish (Ezek. 17:24).

HOPE BECOMES SIGHT

[8] Now while he was serving as priest before God. . . . [11] There appeared to him an angel of the Lord. . . . [13] The angel said to him, "Do not be afraid, Zechariah, for your prayer has been heard, and your wife Elizabeth will bear you a son, and you shall call his name John. . . . [16] He will turn many of the children of Israel to the Lord their God, and he will go before him in the spirit and power of Elijah. . . .

²⁴ After these days his wife Elizabeth conceived, and for five months she kept herself hidden, saying, ²⁵ "Thus the Lord has done for me in the days when he looked on me, to take away my reproach among people." (Luke 1:8–17, 24–25)

Something impossible was about to happen, just as it did for Elizabeth's foremothers Sarah (Gen. 18:11) and Hannah (1 Sam. 1–2). Elizabeth was about to experience the wonder of God doing "far more abundantly than all that we ask or think, according to the power at work within us" (Eph. 3:20).

Priests were chosen by lot to enter the sanctuary of the temple and intercede for God's people. Because there were so many priests, this was often a once-in-a-lifetime event. At just the right moment, God orchestrates the lot to go to Zechariah.

As Zechariah finishes his duties, the angel Gabriel appears and tells him his prayer has been heard. We might think Zechariah's prayer for a child has been heard, but it is likely this was a prayer for God to keep his promise to send Messiah. When Elizabeth and Zechariah realized God would not give them a child, they likely continued to pray for God to send their Redeemer. They lived expectantly, trusting that one day light would shine into the darkness of their world. Hope made their disappointments bearable. It is no coincidence that at this barren time in Israel's history, God used an old, barren couple as the bridge between the old covenant and the ushering in of the new covenant.

When Elizabeth conceived, her emotion-packed response is deeply theological. "Thus the Lord has done for me in the days when he looked on me, to take away my reproach among people" (Luke 1:25).

In the book *Transformed: Life-taker to Life-giver* we read:

> Elizabeth's testimony proclaims the gospel. It seems likely this "daughter of Aaron" was reflecting on the Aaronic blessing.
>
> The LORD bless you and keep you;
>
> The LORD make his face to shine upon you and be gracious to you;
>
> The LORD lift up his countenance upon you and give you peace (Num. 6:24–26).
>
> In Christ, He shines his face upon us and takes away the reproach and guilt of our sin. It must be noted— He can look on us because He looked away from His beloved Son as He bore our sin (Matt. 27:46). Now He looks on us with delight because He looks and sees Jesus.[4]

Elizabeth kept herself hidden for five months. Luke doesn't tell us why, but perhaps she wanted time to hold this precious gift close, to pour over the promises of the coming Messiah and his forerunner, her son. Luke describes Elizabeth as righteous, so we know her life was informed by Scripture.

---

4 Karen Hodge and Susan Hunt, *Transformed: Life-Taker to Life-Giver* (Geanies House, Fearn, Scotland: Christian Focus, 2016), 228.

I suspect she wanted time to pray and ask the Lord to prepare her to better understand his word before relatives and neighbors bombarded her with questions. I envision priceless private days between Elizabeth and the Lord, her heart overflowing with worship and tears streaming down her cheeks in awe of his purposes. I also think this sweet respite prepared her for Mary's arrival.

HOPE SHARED

[39] Mary arose and went with haste into the hill country, to a town in Judah, [40] and she entered the house of Zechariah and greeted Elizabeth. . . . [41] And Elizabeth was filled with the Holy Spirit, [42] and she exclaimed with a loud cry, "Blessed *are* you among women, and blessed *is* the fruit of your womb! [43] And why *is* this *granted* to me that the mother of my Lord should come to me? [44] For behold, when the sound of your greeting came to my ears, the baby in my womb leaped for joy. [45] And blessed *is* she who believed that there would be a fulfillment of what was spoken to her from the Lord."

[46] And Mary said:

"My soul magnifies the Lord,
　　[47] and my spirit rejoices in God my Savior,
[48] for he has looked on the humble estate of his
　　servant." (Luke 1:39–48)

Elizabeth's child would prepare the way for Messiah, and Elizabeth would prepare his young mother. Elizabeth's pregnancy would be the example to remind Mary nothing is impossible with God, and her voice would encourage and equip Mary for her mission. Instead of stooping under the weight of disappointment, she stands tall in her faith, growing sweeter in old age and providing a canopy of gospel refreshment for Mary. This old woman was full of sap and green, ready to welcome Mary and declare God's love, power, and righteousness to her.

Imagine the shock of Elizabeth's neighbors when she ventured out during the sixth month of her pregnancy, and then her relative Mary showed up. Two women. One old, one young. Both experiencing the impossible.

Our anti-aging culture often pushes aside older people to make way for a new generation. This is not God's way. Throughout Scripture, God not only explains the idea of mentoring, but he shows us the power of evergreen, older, wiser people investing in the lives of the next generation. And like Elizabeth and Mary, those relationships are not one-sided. Each generation learns from the other.

For decades Elizabeth daily died to self and twisted herself around the Lord. Her intimacy with him shaped her character and prepared her to encourage and equip Mary to fulfill her mission. She spoke Spirit-led, life-giving words to Mary, words that reveal a grateful, humble heart with no room for jealousy because it is full of God's love. She commends Mary for believing the words of the angel. I suspect these are some of the things Mary stored in her heart and remembered when neighbors or family whispered about her pregnancy or called her son names (Luke 2:19).

It seems the Lord directed Mary to Elizabeth because this young girl needed to be on the fast track of growing even deeper spiritual roots. Elizabeth mothered her young relative for three months, but this was not a one-way relationship. Each time they looked at one another, they remembered that nothing is impossible with God. Each time they heard whispered life-taking words, they could look at each other and smile. Though planted in the mud of scandal, they flourished.

Elizabeth spoke life-giving words, and when Mary sang, she put the testimony of her spiritual mother to verse: "He has looked on the humble estate of his servant" (Luke 1:48).

These women were God-centered, not self-centered.

Elizabeth and Us

Elizabeth's story is our story. Consider the similarities.

Every child of God experiences the impossible when we who were dead in sin are made alive in Christ (Eph. 2:4–5).

Darkness covered Elizabeth's world, culturally, religiously, and personally. We, too, live in darkness until the light of Christ shines into our hearts.

We have all experienced some form of barrenness in our relationships and situations, those times when grief or disappointment cut a devastating swath of death through our lives. Those times are our opportunities to cling in hope to the promise that God can do the impossible and make our parched lives flourish.

"He looked on me" is our testimony (Luke 1:25). God sees us because he has known us since before creation. He removes our reproach through the sacrifice of his Son and sets us free.

We are blameless. "God . . . chose us in [Christ] before the foundation of the world, that we should be holy and blameless before him" (Eph. 1:3–4). He transforms us so we increasingly die to self and become more and more like Jesus. Flourishing in every season and circumstance is possible for the child of God because his Spirit lives in us.

We are called to be involved in covenant community life. Even in old age we can do this by welcoming others and sharing our hope in Jesus with them, offering gospel encouragement and affirmation, and showing the love and kindness of Jesus. Before my then sixty-one-year-old mother received a diagnosis that changed her ability to be actively engaged in church life, she used her big house to welcome young women facing crisis pregnancies to make her home their home. The virus that attacked her heart made it impossible for her to continue offering a safe place for these girls and took away her strength so that she sometimes crawled up the steps to her bedroom. Instead of living out the afternoon of life bike riding and sledding with her grandkids and pouring her life into the teen girls of her church, she had to surrender to a new normal and a better understanding of her identity as a daughter of the King. She struggled to accept how her life could impact others when she was so physically diminished. Yet, until her death thirteen years later, people of all ages and from all walks of life, along with young pastors, frequented her kitchen under the guise of visiting an invalid, but really wanting her encouraging words to help them through difficult responsibilities. They came not because of what she could do, but because her time "planted in the house of the LORD" flowed out onto them (Ps. 92:13). God kept his promise; she bore fruit in old age.

Like Elizabeth, we must daily make the choice to die to self by repenting of bitterness and trusting and obeying God's word, even in disappointing and hard times. My mother's private struggle to understand her new purpose required dying a thousand little deaths.

We, too, must continually remember that when life seems barren, flourishing is possible because "nothing will be impossible with God" (Luke 1:37).

Hope that Jesus is coming makes our disappointments bearable, so we pray, "Come, Lord Jesus!" (Rev. 22:20). Christians today, especially suffering Christians, cling to this promise and look forward to the day when all tears will be wiped away (Rev. 21:4). This world is not all there is. A newly bereaved widow told me the promise of Jesus's return keeps her walking by faith, and she often starts her morning with the words, "Lord, this would be a good day for you to come back."

Shortly after the death of our sixteen-year-old son Mark and his friend, Kelly, in a car accident, Chuck and I heard our seventeen-year-old son Dan wail to a friend, "Jesus needs to come back now. That's the only way this pain will go away."

Such hope and confidence in God's promises fuels our faith and nourishes the spiritual fruit of peace, joy, contentment, and trust in our Father's promise-keeping character, especially when disappointment crashes down. When Mark died, the promise of Jesus's return slowly nurtured our faith, and our barren lives began to show signs of life and joy. God was keeping his promise to bring beauty from ashes; we would flourish as we twisted ourselves around him and his word. God did the impossible in our shattered family.

God is bringing each of his children to eternal glory, but the pathway is one of glory now. He gave me a new heart and adopted me as his daughter. He made me his disciple. He is changing me into Christ's image. He placed me in a strategic position to be a redemptive presence. He promises that as I wait on him, I will flourish until the day I physically die and experience full flourishing.

He is doing the same for each of his children. You might have concluded there is not much in Elizabeth's story for you because it's too late for the Lord to gift you as he did Elizabeth. But wait. A day is coming for each us when our bodies will give out, and for those who don't know Jesus, all will be lost. But for the child of God, light enters that darkness and the darkness cannot overcome it (John 1:5). No child of God dies alone. Like Elizabeth, we look forward to our Savior keeping the promise of his presence in the moment we step from earth to heaven.

> I wait for the LORD, my soul waits,
>> and in his word I hope;
> my soul waits for the Lord
>> more than watchmen for the morning
>>> (Ps. 130:5–6).

Sherry's Story

Sherry Bitler is a seventy-year-old wife, mother, grandmother, and founder of a traditional Christian school, a homeschool cooperative, and a summer program for children at a Christian conference center. She lives in Middletown, Delaware.

After a diagnosis of multiple sclerosis, I took early retirement and left a twenty-five-year ministry to children. I immediately missed everything about the large program, school, and staff, but also looked forward to spending more time with our grandchildren. However, as I struggled with the potential progressive physical limitations of MS, all I could see in my future was a wheelchair and total dependence on my family for the most basic needs. I desperately needed to find a way to be useful, to flourish in these new chapters of my story. Discouragement drove me to pray Psalm 71:18: "So even to old age and gray hairs, / O God, do not forsake me, / until I proclaim your might to another generation, / your power to all those to come."

The Lord responded with this promise from Isaiah 46:4: "Even to your old age I am he, / and to gray hairs I will carry you, / I have made, and I will bear; / I will carry and will save."

This scripture gave me confidence that God would strengthen me to find ways to keep investing in others. My favorite large group events became ideas for interacting in small groups. The children's conferences for one hundred became Cousins Camp for our grandchildren. Bible study for fifty women became small groups of ten young moms around my dining room table. I now had time to experience the incredible blessing of one-on-one relationships. As the Lord put specific women on my mind, I scheduled monthly visits with friends who needed a safe place: an acquaintance diagnosed with MS years earlier, a spiritual mother who recently lost her only daughter during brain surgery, a widowed friend, and a pastor's wife who needed a friend outside her small congregation. Our pool and fenced-yard became a perfect setting for Wednesday pool days for young moms and their children.

Because of my physical and energy limitations, I plan my time carefully. Some days the price is pain or complete exhaustion, so I schedule rest days. I continue to ask God to help me discern when to persevere and when to accept my limitations. My heart's desire is to flourish even as I continue aging. I want to use the energy God gives me to encourage others, giving all the credit to him. Remembering that God is lovingly writing my story gives me great peace and purpose.

Questions for Reflection and Discussion

1. Hope in God's promises fueled Elizabeth's response to her barrenness. Read Luke 1:5–7 and Romans 15:4. What was Elizabeth's hope? What is yours?

2. As Elizabeth twisted herself around God's word, she learned how to do what feels impossible in the middle of deep sadness. Where does it feel impossible for you to die to self in order to flourish? For hopeful encouragement, meditate on Genesis 18:14; Psalm 25:3; Psalm 39:7; Isaiah 40:31; Luke 18:27; and Luke 1:36–37.

3. How does Elizabeth's story encourage you to believe you can flourish in whatever circumstances God places you?

7

The Long View
Psalm 71

SUSAN

Elizabeth Prentiss, nineteenth-century author of *Stepping Heavenward*, wrote to a friend: "I'm ever so glad that I'm growing old every day, and so becoming better fitted to be the dear and loving friend to young people I want to be."[1]

This quote is countercultural and counterintuitive—it values aging and is not self-centered. Mrs. Prentiss was thinking biblically and living covenantally. Throughout the Old Testament we are told that "one generation shall commend your works to another" (Ps. 145:4).

---

1   George Prentiss, *More Love to Thee: The Life and Letters of Elizabeth Prentiss* (Amityville, NY: Calvary Press, 1994), 280.

I think Mrs. Prentiss expressed the same heart-posture as the writer of Psalm 71. The author is not named, but commentators agree it is the prayer of an old man. Many think it is likely David's prayer at the time of the insurrection of his son Absalom—a sordid story of rape, murder, and conspiracy blowing up any facade of family unity (2 Sam. 13–18). Yet, this is a prayer of one who is flourishing in old age. It may sound extreme, but I think it's true: there is no growing in grace apart from prayer.

A Prayer of the Aged for the Ages

PSALM 71:1–4

> ¹ In you, O LORD, do I take refuge;
>> let me never be put to shame!
> ² In your righteousness deliver me and rescue me;
>> incline your ear to me, and save me!
> ³ Be to me a rock of refuge,
>> to which I may continually come;
> you have given the command to save me,
>> for you are my rock and my fortress.
> ⁴ Rescue me, O my God, from the hand of the
>> wicked,
>> from the grasp of the unjust and cruel man.

Remember the painful context, and reflect on the following characteristics of this psalmist's prayer:

- Submission to God's will
- Tender intimacy with God—note the personal pronouns.
- Knowledge of and trust in God's character.
- Hope in God.
- Continual praise.

Scripture tells us, "Wisdom is with the aged, / and understanding in length of days" (Job 12:12). Biblical wisdom increases the longer we know and trust Jesus. Length of days gives a long-view perspective of the redemption story God writes in our lives. From my eighty-year-old perspective I can now look back and see that nothing was random; nothing was wasted. God used, and continues to use, everything—my sin, the sin of others against me, the disappointments, sorrows, grief, suffering, times of rejoicing, and times of weeping—to shape me into his image. I would not change anything because each thing drew me nearer to him.

David is not paralyzed by feeling failure as a parent or the shame of this public rejection, because his hope is not grounded in people or circumstances. His reference point and refuge is God. A refuge is a place of safety and protection, a sanctuary. David thinks and acts biblically. He flees to God in prayer. "We who have fled [to God] for refuge might have strong encouragement to hold fast to the hope set before us. We have this as a sure and steadfast anchor of the soul, a hope that enters into the inner place behind the curtain, where Jesus has gone" (Heb. 6:18–20).

Growing in Grace

There is no age, sin, or suffering that negates the prayer promise of Hebrews 4:14–16: "Since then we have a great high priest who has passed through the heavens, Jesus, the Son of God, . . . Let us then with confidence draw near to the throne of grace, that we may receive mercy and find grace to help in time of need." If we are in Christ, we have access to the inner place behind the curtain where we find grace to grow and flourish in every relationship and situation.

REMEMBERING

David begins to reminisce, a favorite activity of the elderly. John Calvin wrote that Psalm 71 shows "the powerful influence which the remembrance of God's benefits had in nourishing his hope."[2]

Pastor George Grant writes:

One of the hazards of the fall is forgetfulness. All of us need regular reminders of the truth of God's Word and the fidelity of His character in order to persevere in our callings. . . . And that is why the ministry of the Holy

2 John Calvin, *Commentary on the Book of Psalms*, vol. 3 (Grand Rapids, MI: Eerdmans, 1949), 84.

Spirit in the lives of believers is primarily to bring to our remembrance the Word of Truth (John 14:26). . . . He calls on us to reflect on all that He has done so that everything that we are now called to do and everything that we are now called to be takes the shape of His purposes and not merely ours.[3]

Mama was ninety-nine when she died. Her memory was sharp to the last day. Our children and grandchildren were fascinated with the things she remembered, and Mama loved telling stories. In her last years her perspective became more pronounced. Even when she talked about the Great Depression, or all her brothers serving in World War II, or the hardships when she and Daddy lost the farm and moved to a new place to start a new business, she always said, "It was hard, but God made it all turn out good." Mama remembered God's benefits, as David did when he talked to his own soul.

> Bless the LORD, O my soul,
>   and forget not all his benefits,
> who forgives all your iniquity,
>   who heals all your diseases,
> who redeems your life from the pit,
>   who crowns you with steadfast love [*hesed*] and
>   mercy,

3   George Grant, quoted in *Life-Giving Leadership*, Karen Hodge and Susan Hunt (Lawrenceville, GA: Committee on Discipleship Ministries, 2018), 174.

who satisfies you with good
 so that your youth is renewed like the eagle's.
  (Ps. 103:2–5)

Growing in Grace

Thinking biblically means thinking big and long—thinking big thoughts about God and praying for spiritual eyes to see his long story of redemption being written in our lives.

Remembering His Youth

PSALM 71:5–8

⁵ For you, O Lord, are my hope,
  my trust, O LORD, from my youth.
⁶ Upon you I have leaned from before my birth;
  you are he who took me from my mother's
   womb.
My praise is continually of you.
⁷ I have been as a portent to many,
  but you are my strong refuge.
⁸ My mouth is filled with your praise,
  and with your glory all the day.

Remembering God's character inspires David to declare God's sovereignty and his hope (*tikvah*). *Lord, Adonai,* means "master," the one who has all authority. *LORD,* or

Yahweh, is his personal name of covenant faithfulness and steadfast love (*hesed*). Our knowledge of God reminds us that he formed us in our mothers' wombs and gave us our first breath and every breath since that moment. We are "his workmanship" (Eph. 2:10). Before we knew God, he knew and loved us (Eph. 1:4–5).

Growing in Grace

Going behind the curtain where Jesus is, and remembering his covenant faithfulness and love, ignites hope and fuels praise—elements of flourishing.

Remembering Midlife

PSALM 71:9–14

> ⁹ Do not cast me off in the time of old age;
>
>> forsake me not when my strength is spent.
>
> ¹⁰ For my enemies speak concerning me;
>
>> those who watch for my life consult together
>
> ¹¹ and say, "God has forsaken him;
>
>> pursue and seize him,
>>
>> for there is none to deliver him."
>
> ¹² O God, be not far from me;
>
>> O my God, make haste to help me!
>
> ¹³ May my accusers be put to shame and consumed;
>
>> with scorn and disgrace may they be covered
>>
>> who seek my hurt.

¹⁴ But I will hope continually
and will praise you yet more and more.

Many commentators suggest these verses refer to the middle portion of David's life, which was characterized by enemies, battles, and successes. I asked a group of midlife women what characterizes their lives. Their words included *busy*, *stretched*, *cuteness* (babies), *chaos* (teens), *careers*, *transitions*, *tired*.

Looking back fortifies David to face the realities of old-age weakness, suffering, and sorrow. Perhaps he remembers that when he walked through valleys of death, God was with him (Ps. 23). The Lord was always the stronghold of his life (Ps. 27), the one who even used the sin of his adultery and murder to teach him about the grace of repentance and the mercy of forgiveness and restoration (Ps. 51).

A long view helps us see God's gracious hand of providence weaving everything together for his glory and our good. The Westminster Larger Catechism explains: "God's works of providence are his most holy, wise, and powerful preserving and governing all his creatures; ordering them, and all their actions, to his own glory."[4]

Psalm 71:14 is a testimony of how remembering results in an unbroken hope and a mature praise.

4   *Westminster Larger Catechism*, question 18.

Growing in Grace

We flourish in old age when we look back and praise the Lord that all things worked together according to his purpose to make us more like Jesus, and nothing ever separated us from his love (Rom. 8:28–39). This long view of the redemptive story God is writing in our lives equips us to help the younger generation see the beauty and significance of each part of their story.

Remembering Our Mission

PSALM 71:15–18

¹⁵ My mouth will tell of your righteous acts,
　　of your deeds of salvation all the day,
　　　for their number is past my knowledge.
¹⁶ With the mighty deeds of the Lord GOD [a
　　　　combination of *Adonai* and *Yahweh*] I will come;
　　I will remind them of your righteousness, yours
　　　　alone.
¹⁷ O God, from my youth you have taught me,
　　and I still proclaim your wondrous deeds.
¹⁸ So even to old age and gray hairs,
　　O God, do not forsake me,
until I proclaim your might to another generation,
　　your power to all those to come.

A living hope fixed on Christ makes us missional even in old age. David's son rejects him, but David still wants to proclaim God's righteousness, authority, and covenant love to the next generation. His son may not listen, but there are those who will, and there are those who will listen to you.

The generational principle is expanded in Jesus's Great Commission to disciple the nations (Matt. 28:18–20) and echoed in Titus 2:3–5: "Older women . . . are to teach what is good, and so train the young women." Declaring the gospel to the next generation is a characteristic of living covenantally. We can be life-giving spiritual mothers even, and perhaps especially, in old age.[5] I no longer have the physical or mental energy to teach a weekly Bible study, but here are a few ways I'm learning to be missional in this season.

The privilege of prayer. I love Paul's mother imagery in Galatians 4:19: "My little children, for whom I am again in the anguish of childbirth until Christ is formed in you!" They were Christians, but Paul longed for Christ to be formed— to grow bigger—in them. There is much we cannot do, but we can labor in prayer for the formation of Christ in the lives of those entrusted to us. I never knew my great-grandmother Cassie, but since I was a girl I heard about her love for Jesus and that she prayed for her children and for the generations to come. I am an answer to her prayers, and now my prayers mingle with hers as I pray for the generations to come.

The power of Scripture. A young mama in our church was facing cancer surgery. Women were mobilizing to take care of

---

5 See Susan Hunt's *Spiritual Mothering: The Titus 2 Model for Women Mentoring Women* (Wheaton, IL: Crossway, 1992) and *Titus 2 Tools* (Lawrenceville, GA: PCA Committee on Discipleship Ministries, 2016), a manual with suggestions for implementing Titus 2 discipleship in the local church.

her practical needs, but I was not physically able to help. Finally I told her my frustration and asked if there was anything I could do. She smiled and said, "Yes. My mind is so scattered I cannot think what Scriptures to read. Will you send me some verses?" I was immediately on it, emailing some verses, and then texting a verse each morning. She repeatedly told me how the verses helped her deal with fear and gave her comfort and peace. We both flourished, and so did our friendship.

When our grandchildren were little, Gene and I memorized Scripture with them. Now they are busy young adults, so we text them a Scripture verse every morning, and we ask the Holy Spirit to produce his fruit in their lives.

Stewarding our marriage. Gene and I are overwhelmed with God's gift of a long and happy marriage. We pray we will be good stewards of this gift and show our grandchildren and the young couples in our church that, by God's grace, marriage can grow sweeter each day.

The fruitfulness of one-on-one conversations. For years I coordinated a women's ministry. I loved it, but it left little time for couch conversations—just sitting and talking. Twenty-five years ago these conversations would have been laced with solutions. Now, with a grateful nod to William Cowper, my conversations with young women are guided by his deep reflections on God's providence as expressed in his hymn "God Moves in a Mysterious Way." Here is a sampling of these conversations.

"No one prepares you for how hard marriage and parenting are. When our spouses and children disappoint us, it's easy to feel self-pity and sadness. When our kids are mistreated or upset, it affects us. I know Scripture says to trust the Lord and find joy in him, but it's hard. The struggle is real! How can I be a life-giver while dealing with the realities of marriage and parenthood?"

> God moves in a mysterious way his wonders to
> > perform;
> he plants his footsteps in the sea, and rides upon the
> > storm.

"I do not feel as if I'm flourishing; I'm just existing. My relationships, with a couple exceptions, are one-sided. My marriage is not bad, but it's not alive or vibrant. I seldom feel wanted (needed—yes; everyone needs me to do things for them) or known simply for who I am. I try to press on by reading my Bible, but I still feel as though I just continue like a plant with green leaves and sap but no blooms or fruit."

> Deep in unfathomable mines of never-failing skill
> he treasures up his bright designs, and works his
> > sovereign will.

"My adult children's choices break my heart. From the time they were born, I protected them. Now I can't control what they do, so I can't protect them from the consequences of their choices. I want to stay strong and finish well, but I'm emotionally exhausted."

Ye fearful saints, fresh courage take; the clouds ye so
    much dread
are big with mercy, and shall break in blessings on your
    head.

"It's hard to believe my husband left me after almost three decades of marriage. Last night was difficult. I fixated on what he did rather than on Jesus and what he has done and is doing."

Judge not the Lord by feeble sense, but trust him for his
    grace;
behind a frowning providence he hides a smiling face.

"I'm almost fifty. My job is boring. The women gossip and manipulate. How can I be a life-giver when they are sucking the life out of me?"

His purposes will ripen fast, unfolding ev'ry hour;
the bud may have a bitter taste, but sweet will be the flow'r.[6]

These conversations feel familiar because they remind me of situations Jesus used to wean me from relying on myself to fix everyone and everything and woo me to trust his providence. It has taken decades for me to learn to be still, and know that he is God (Ps. 46:10) and that "in quietness and in trust shall be [my] strength" (Isa. 30:15). One joy of aging is a stillness of soul that helps us see the small moments as sacred moments when we can reflect God's glory to someone else. I often encourage young women to watch for heavenly

6   William Cowper, "God Moves in a Mysterious Way," 1774.

hugs—those seemingly ordinary things like a kind word or deed at just the moment we need it—and to praise God for his tender care. Length of days prepares us to help younger people see and trust God's sovereign providence in their lives. Sometimes I ask questions to help women think biblically and live covenantally.

What is your reference point as you evaluate this relationship/situation?

What is your authority—the Bible or your feelings?

What will it mean for you to submit to God's authority and glorify him as a life-giver?

Are you willing to repent of any ways you are being a life-taker?

What will it cost you to die to self?

What can I do to help you?

Growing in Grace

When we put down the pen, stop trying to write our story or the stories of others, and wholeheartedly trust the author of our story to write his gospel story in our lives, we begin to see the mundane and the miserable moments as essential sentences that eventually become a majestic story of grace, because the plot of dirt where we die is also the place where we flourish.

Anticipating Future Glory

PSALM 71:19–24

> [19] Your righteousness, O God,
>> reaches the high heavens.
> You who have done great things,
>> O God, who is like you?
> [20] You who have made me see many troubles and
>> calamities
> will revive me again;
> from the depths of the earth
>> you will bring me up again.
> [21] You will increase my greatness
>> and comfort me again.
> [22] I will also praise you with the harp
>> for your faithfulness, O my God;
> I will sing praises to you with the lyre,
>> O Holy One of Israel.
> [23] My lips will shout for joy,
>> when I sing praises to you;
>> my soul also, which you have redeemed.
> [24] And my tongue will talk of your righteous help all
>> the day long,
> for they have been put to shame and disappointed
>> who sought to do me hurt.

Remembering God's sovereign providence and love takes us full circle to where we began—worship. It is because God does all things right that the juxtaposition of him causing the "great things" *and* the "many troubles and calamities" is comforting and not bewildering. It all works together to accomplish God's purpose in our life. David looks ahead to the resurrection with hope and joy. We shortchange the beautiful concept of flourishing unless we acknowledge that full flourishing comes at physical death. J. I. Packer wrote, "Dying well is one of the good works to which Christians are called, and Christ will enable us who serve him to die well, however gruesome the physical process itself. And dying thus, in Christ, through Christ, and with Christ, will be a spiritual blossoming."[7]

Tim Keller explains:

> The Christian hope is a hope that you're going to get the life you always wanted. . . . Our Christian hope is that we're going to live with Christ in a new earth, where there is not only no more death, but where life is what it was always meant to be. . . . Our character and daily life are shaped by what we believe about our ultimate future.[8]

And Charles Spurgeon sums it up: "Those who die daily will die easily.[9]

When David was told that Absalom died in battle he lamented, "O my son Absalom, my son, my son Absalom!

---

7 J. I. Packer, "Only When You Know How to Die Can You Know How to Live," in *O Love That Will Not Let Me Go*, ed. Nancy Guthrie (Wheaton, IL: Crossway, 2011), 15.

8 Tim Keller, "Rubbing Hope into the Reality of Suffering," in *O Love That Will Not Let Me Go*, 90.

9 Charles Haddon Spurgeon, "Those Who Die Daily Die Easily," in *O Love That Will Not Let Me Go*, 149.

Would I had died instead of you!" (2 Sam 18:33). But David could not take his son's place. There is only one who could take our place and be our substitute.

Growing in Grace

We flourish when we bow in submission and gratitude to the one "who was delivered up for our transgressions and raised for our justification" (Rom. 4:25) and look with expectation to the appointed day of our glorification.

Psalm 71 shows us the power of the gospel to break through and out-distance our sin, shame, sorrow, and suffering, to draw us into greater intimacy with Jesus, and to motivate us to "talk of [God's] righteous help all the day long" (v. 24). It shows the power of prayer to anchor our soul. In one of her last letters, Elizabeth Prentiss, who suffered ill-health and the death of children, wrote: "Much of my experiences of life has cost me a great price and I wish to use it for strengthening and comforting other souls."[10] Her hymn is the prayer of a flourishing, growing, fruitful heart.

> More love to thee, O Christ, more love to thee!
> Hear thou the prayer I make on bended knee;
> this is my earnest plea, more love, O Christ, to thee,
> more love to thee, more love to thee!

10 Prentiss, *More Love to Thee*, preface.

Once earthly joy I craved, sought peace and rest;
now thee alone I seek; give what is best;
this all my prayer shall be, more love, O Christ, to
    thee . . .

Let sorrow do its work, send grief and pain;
sweet are thy messengers, sweet their refrain,
when they can sing with me, more love, O Christ to
    thee . . .

Then shall my latest breath whisper thy praise;
this be the parting cry my heart shall raise,
this still its prayer shall be, more love, O Christ, to
    thee . . .[11]

Carol's Story

Carol Arnold has four children, twelve grandchildren, and four great-grandchildren and lives in Orlando, Florida. She serves with Equipping Pastors International, a mission organization founded by her husband, Jack.

"Never say never!"

I was married to a man in ministry for forty-seven years. He wasn't a Boy Scout. He didn't like surprises. Or adventures. Or flying—he was six foot three and didn't fit in airline seats. I grew up camping, riding horses, trying weird foods, and moving to Guam when I was ten. I loved adventure.

11 Elizabeth Payson Prentiss, "More Love to Thee, O Christ," 1869.

If you had asked me when I was a young pastor's wife with four boys, without much money and no extra time, what would be my dream in life, I would have said, "To travel the world and teach women God's word." Obviously it would never happen, because my husband hated to travel.

But here I am, eighty-two years old, a widow of fourteen years, traveling the world and teaching women. And I did it *with* my husband the last nine years of his life; he was never happier.

Between the time we married and our last years of marriage, there were wilderness years when I was a life-taker to my husband. I loved being a mother, but I did not love being a wife. That time felt like wasted years, but in that wilderness God lovingly prepared, taught, broke, and changed me. He gave me the message he planned for me to share with others. My failure to be the wife my husband needed, and how God changed me rather than me trying to change my husband, is now the main theme of my ministry to women around the world. To me, flourishing means gratefully accepting the past and present trials God gives me, and looking for opportunities to use what I have learned to help others.

My passion now is to encourage others to see the powerful ministry of marriage—the picture God has given of the relationship between Christ and his church. The enemy hates this picture and will do whatever it takes to damage and destroy it. Marriages are in trouble all over the world. As an older woman, I can give a perspective that younger men and women need in order to persevere.

Whatever situations we find ourselves in as we age, there are nuggets of gold in our past that we can pass on to others. God never wastes a trial, a grief, or a wilderness wandering. We flourish when we give to others the lessons God has taught us.

Questions for Reflection and Discussion

1. Which *Growing in Grace* principle is especially helpful to you at this point in your life and why?

2. Spend time remembering God's benefits. Think big and long about God's redemption story in your life.

3. Summarize what you have learned from this chapter.

8

Naomi
Ruth 1–4

SHARON

In our quest to understand what aging with grace looks like, we have looked to women who have gone before us for examples of flourishing.

Anna: holding onto hope, worshiping, and serving God's people.

The matriarchs: choosing to die to self for the sake of the next generation.

Elizabeth: physically barren, yet in full bloom.

And now Naomi: widowed, empty, and then full and flourishing.

At first read, it may seem that the book of Ruth is a beautiful record of the love story of Ruth and Boaz. And it is. But it is also an even more beautiful and life-transforming story of the love between God and Naomi. Though the main characters do not know it, their story shows us one more step in God's plan to redeem his people through his Son, Jesus, of the line of David. The master storyteller weaves the theme of *hesed* (his loyal love for us) throughout, and in so doing leads us to the heart of the gospel message. Sinclair Ferguson says, "This covenanted commitment is a central theme in the Old Testament and forms the melody line of the book of Ruth."[1]

Naomi's story is our story.

Naomi's Story

[1] In the days when the judges ruled there was a famine in the land, and a man of Bethlehem in Judah went to sojourn in the country of Moab, he and his wife and his two sons. [2] The name of the man was Elimelech and the name of his wife Naomi, and the names of his two sons were Mahlon and Chilion. They were Ephrathites from Bethlehem in Judah. They went into the country of Moab and remained there. [3] But Elimelech, the husband of Naomi, died. . . . [4] [Her sons] took Moabite wives; the name of the one was Orpah and the name of the other Ruth. They lived there about ten years, [5] and both Mahlon and Chilion died, so that the woman was left without her two sons and her husband. (Ruth 1:1–5)

1 Sinclair Ferguson, *Faithful God: An Exposition of the Book of Ruth* (Wales, UK: Bryntirion Press, 2005), 64.

Naomi lived in the time of the judges. The book of Judges tells the national story of a dark period of Israel's history and ends with this startling statement: "In those days there was no king in Israel. Everyone did what was right in his own eyes" (Judg. 21:25). In the book of Ruth, God tells how he wrote his redemption story into the life of one family during this time of spiritual darkness. Naomi did not know her ordinary little family would become an extraordinary link to the coming Messiah. In fact, she died without knowing how her seemingly insignificant life fit into God's magnificent eternal tapestry.

Naomi's story begins with what some conclude were sinful choices that led to loss, death, emptiness, and despair; it ends in fullness, life, and joy. The Hebrew root word for *widow* is *alem*, which means "unable to speak." Though viewed by herself and others as a useless, burdensome old woman, God reverses the status of this voiceless widow and makes her a critical piece of his gospel story, as he did for many marginalized women throughout Scripture and throughout history.

This ancient story has incredible contemporary parallels to us. Losing a spouse and/or a child are major human stressors.[2] Naomi's other losses were tortuous as well. Her sedate life changed when a famine invaded their hometown and Elimilech moved his family from Bethlehem ("House of Bread") to Moab so they could eat. They knew famine

---

2   See the Holmes-Rahe stress scale, an inventory of stressful life events.

was God's discipline for disobedience (Deut. 28), yet like Abraham before them (Gen. 12:10) they concluded Yahweh could not feed them in a famine, so they moved out from under a discipline designed to turn hearts back to Yahweh and depended on a godless country for food. Imagine Naomi's anxiety when she could not feed her children enough and the uncertainty when they moved to a country saturated with false gods, leaving behind family and friends. Then, in this unfamiliar land, Elimilech died, her sons chose Moabite women as wives (a Jewish mother's worst nightmare; Deut. 23:3–6), and a decade later her sons died, leaving childless widows. Pause for a moment and consider the tsunami of grief that must have swallowed up Naomi's life.

Returning Home

⁶ Then she arose with her daughters-in-law to return . . . for she had heard . . . that the LORD had visited his people and given them food. . . . ⁸ But Naomi said to her two daughters-in-law, "Go, return each of you to her mother's house. May the LORD deal kindly with you, as you have dealt with the dead and with me. ⁹ The LORD grant that you may find rest, each of you in the house of her husband!" Then she kissed them, and they lifted up their voices and wept. ¹⁰ And they said to her, "No, we will return with you to your people." ¹¹ But Naomi said, "Turn back, my daughters. . . . ¹³ It is exceedingly bitter to me for your sake that the hand of the LORD has gone

out against me." [14] . . . Orpah kissed her mother-in-law, but Ruth clung to her. . . .

[16] Ruth said, "Do not urge me to leave you or to return from following you. For where you go I will go, and where you lodge I will lodge. Your people shall be my people, and your God my God. [17] Where you die I will die, and there will I be buried. May the LORD do so to me and more also if anything but death parts me from you."

[19] . . . And when they came to Bethlehem, the whole town was stirred because of them. And the women said, "Is this Naomi?" [20] She said to them, "Do not call me Naomi; call me Mara, for the Almighty has dealt very bitterly with me. [21] I went away full, and the LORD has brought me back empty. Why call me Naomi, when the LORD has testified against me and the Almighty has brought calamity upon me?" (Ruth 1:6–21)

In God's providence, Naomi heard he had visited his people and the famine was over. She declares God had testified against her, but her prayer for Orpah and Ruth reveals a spark of hope in her soul (Ruth 1:8–9, 21). Naomi had been planted in the house of the Lord. She remembers, and she returns home.

Orpah made a common-sense decision. Ruth made a faith decision. In this profound moment, Ruth pleaded with Naomi to understand that she now embraced Naomi's God as her own, and she promised to never leave Naomi, thus voluntarily pledging her life to Yahweh and to her mother-in-law. Is it possible Ruth's words reminded brokenhearted Naomi of

God's covenant promise and everlasting love? "Know therefore that the LORD your God is God, the faithful God who keeps covenant and steadfast love with those who love him and keep his commandments, to a thousand generations" (Deut. 7:9).

Naomi set her sights on Bethlehem. Traveling during this godless period was dangerous under normal circumstances, but two women traveling alone were at even greater risk. Their trip took seven to ten days on rough terrain, with no street lights, a river crossing, and a climb up a two-thousand-foot elevation, finally arriving in Bethlehem. The townswomen wondered aloud if the old woman with the young Gentile was Naomi. Naomi's response acknowledges her understanding of God's sovereignty: "The LORD has brought me back empty" (Ruth 1:21).

Naomi believed God was sovereign, but pain filled every part of her being and seemed to crowd out any vestiges of God's love. Even more devastating than the deaths of her husband and sons was her disconnect with God's *hesed*.

HESED FLOWS FROM GOD TO US

Translators find it difficult to adequately define *hesed* in English. It is one of the most powerful and richest words in Scripture. Translations like "enduring love," "everlasting love," "faithful love," "eternal love," "mercy," "kindness," and "everlasting kindness" fall short of plumbing the depths of God's *hesed*. *Hesed* is a voluntary commitment and unbreakable pledge to act for the good of another in spite of emotions, often at great personal sacrifice.

God declared *hesed* for his people when he passed by Moses on the mountain: "The LORD passed before him and proclaimed, 'The LORD, the LORD, a God merciful and gracious, slow to anger, and abounding in steadfast love and faithfulness [*hesed*], keeping steadfast love [*hesed*] for thousands, forgiving iniquity and transgression and sin'" (Ex. 34:6–7).

No betrayal or sin is beyond the healing power of God's persistent and enduring *hesed*:

> For the Lord will not cast off forever,
> but, though he cause grief, he will have compassion,
>   according to the abundance of his steadfast love
>   [*hesed*]. (Lam. 3:31–32)

No matter how devastating life's circumstances may be, God's love never quits:

> For the mountains may depart
>   and the hills be removed,
> but my steadfast love [*hesed*] shall not depart from you.
>   (Isa. 54:10)

Notice the similarities between Ruth's promise to Naomi and God's promise to the Israelites: "Be strong and courageous. Do not fear or be in dread of them, for it is the LORD your God who goes with you. He will not leave you or forsake you" (Deut. 31:6).

Hesed is not just an Old Testament concept. In the New Testament we see God's loyal love to faithless and undeserving people on full display through the sacrifice of his only Son, Jesus. His love relentlessly pursues his children. His love never quits. We see God's ultimate *hesed* in the cross. Jesus's last words on earth repeat the promise of God's everlasting presence that is inherent in his promise of *hesed*: "And behold, *I am with you always*, to the end of the age" (Matt. 28:20).

Because of God's *hesed* revealed through the life, death, resurrection, and ascension of Jesus, we can "with confidence draw near to the throne of grace, that we may receive mercy and find grace to help in time of need" (Heb. 4:14–16). When life doesn't make sense, we can read our Bible and find story after story of God's *hesed* and know we can trust him because he promises his loyal love to us.

Hesed seems impossible for humans to offer to other humans, yet *hesed*, practiced by Ruth and Boaz, was used by God to pull Naomi's heart toward him.

HESED FLOWS FROM US TO OTHERS

In the remainder of the story we see God's providence gently orchestrating events so that Ruth gleans in the fields of Boaz, a relative of Naomi who could be Ruth's legal kinsman-redeemer, a legal protection that restored a widow's rights and legacy (Deut. 25:5–6). Naomi instructs Ruth how to seek marriage with Boaz. After exploring all other possible legal suitors, Boaz agrees to marry Ruth. They conceive a son and name him Obed, who became the grandfather of the future King David.

The word *hesed* appears three times in Ruth (1:8; 2:20; 3:10), but the practice of *hesed* shows up repeatedly, through mundane and major actions, often in the context of prayer.

- The responses of Orpah and Ruth when Naomi told them to go back to their mothers indicates Naomi intentionally extended *hesed* to these girls, even though they were not Jewish (Ruth 1:9–10).
- Naomi practiced *hesed* when she prayed for Orpah and Ruth (1:8). The needs of her daughters-in-law took precedence over her own at great personal cost. If they listened to her, she would be alone.
- Ruth demonstrated *hesed* when she made a voluntary commitment to Naomi (1:16–17).
- Boaz declared that Ruth practiced *hesed* when she refused to leave Naomi and promised to care for her (2:11–13).
- Naomi recognized *hesed* in the amount of grain Ruth brought home and declared that Boaz extended lovingkindness to this young widow (2:20).
- Ruth deployed *hesed* when she repeatedly humbled herself and prioritized care for her mother-in-law, no matter the personal cost (2:3).
- Boaz's response to Ruth when she risked her reputation to come to him on the threshing floor was an act of *hesed* (3:10).

- Boaz modeled *hesed* when he became a kinsman-redeemer for Ruth at personal financial risk to himself (Deut. 25:5–6).
- The women of Bethlehem praised Ruth for her *hesed* in bearing a son for Naomi (Ruth 4:14–17).

God created us as his image bearers. When we voluntarily commit ourselves to extend loyal love to another, a love generated by God's grace and driven by our commitment not emotion, others catch a glimpse of God's *hesed*. This is not about outward behavior. This is an inner transformation accomplished by God's Spirit. When *hesed* flourishes in our hearts, it flows out to others.

Naomi and Us

Naomi's story is a beautiful picture of the gospel. God relentlessly pursued Naomi. Unbeknownst to her, in the middle of her tragedies, he was preparing a safe place for her under the care of a kinsman-redeemer, Boaz. Likewise, Jesus, our Kinsman-Redeemer, pursues us and is preparing a place for us (John 14:2).

Naomi lamented yet she did not forget to pray. Her faith decision meant returning home, perhaps hoping she would find not only physical bread but spiritual healing. Naomi's return was a scary journey. She returned empty. Dear friend, are you bitter because loved ones neglect you? Are you irritable because of chronic pain? Are you unforgiving of past wrongs done to you? Are you fearful because God does not seem near? I think Naomi would urge you not to languish in the far place; instead, pray. Return home by acknowledging and repenting of your sin. Ask Jesus to empty you of yourself and fill you with his lovingkindness.

God used other people to show his *hesed* to Naomi. Their kindness fanned into flame sparks of hope hiding in Naomi's soul. God did not draw Naomi back to him with thunder and lightning, shaming, condemnation, or long speeches rebuking her for her faith struggles. He showed Naomi his love through the quiet, consistent, self-sacrificing loyal love of Ruth. With each act of Ruth's self-denial, light started chasing away the darkness. Be watchful to see God extending his *hesed* to you through the kindness of others. Be alert to opportunities you have to show kindness to others, and watch your darkness be trampled by the light of Jesus our Redeemer (John 1:5).

Naomi acted covenantally, discipling Ruth and seeking a kinsman-redeemer to redeem her inheritance. God filled Naomi's emptiness with his gladness through the birth of a child. Many of us experience circumstances that tempt us to isolate. Naomi's message to us is clear. Live covenantally. Stay connected to our covenant family. We, too, can be glad because of the birth of a child, the Christ child.

It is an "aha moment" when we realize the book of Ruth is not about Ruth or Naomi. It is about God relentlessly pursuing his eternal plan of salvation. This story is about the glory of God. We can be confident God is moving through our lives in a similar way.

Sinclair Ferguson explains:

God does not mean to touch only *our* lives by what he does in us; he has the lives of others in view—even those yet unborn. That is why life can seem so untidy for the people of God. He has not yet finished his business. There may be many loose ends. The tapestry is only partially complete. He has still much weaving to do in which he will bring these loose ends together, perhaps in someone else's life in the future—long after we are gone. God means to bring blessings and answers to prayer beyond anything we could ever ask or imagine—just as he did here. As Hebrews chapter 11 makes clear, it is a mark of genuine faith to look beyond our own day to the time when God will fulfill his promises.[3]

As we age and face loss after loss, perhaps living our last years in a small room, surrounded by medical supplies and machines, we may wonder how it is possible our lives could be part of God's eternal plan. Buried deep within the heart of a child of God is an unbreakable hope and an everlasting love. Our audience may be only caregivers, nurses, or doctors, but they can leave our presence touched by our trust in God's presence and loyal love.

O the Deep, Deep Love of Jesus

I love Naomi's transparency. She believed in God's sovereignty, but her deep grief over the deaths of her husband and sons led her to conclude that God had broken his promise of *hesed*. I can relate.

3 Ferguson, *Faithful God*, 145.

Shortly after Mark's death, I wrote in my journal, "Sometimes I feel as though I've not only lost Mark, I've lost my relationship to the Lord. I don't know how to reconcile his love with his sovereignty, and that is sometimes even more frightening than my grief over Mark."

I knew I would never again hug our youngest child, ruffle his dark, curly hair, or hear him say, "I love you, too, Mom." Like Naomi, I knew the history of God's faithfulness to his people and specifically to me. I loved singing hymns of God's love. Like Naomi, I also believed in God's sovereignty, although it was not a comfort to me in the days following Mark's death. With Naomi, I said, "I was once full, now I'm empty. God knew when he gave us Mark, he would take him back sixteen years later." And yet, also like Naomi, my prayers revealed a desperate longing to experience his love once more. Something in Naomi, something in me, would not allow us to forget God's faithful love. Like little children furious because we couldn't have our way, we still reached to our faithful God with open arms, hoping he would pick us up and hold us tightly. We forgot for a little while that we were already held tightly in his grip and his *hesed* would not allow him to let us go.

When I wrestled to reconcile God's sovereignty with his love, he sent his people to be his promise keepers.[4] On an especially dark day when the ache in my chest refused to

4   For more examples of how God's people were his promises keepers, see *Treasures of Encouragement: Women Helping Women in the Church* (Phillipsburg, NJ: P&R), Kindle ed.

break, God moved a friend to send me a note with this scripture: "He has said, 'I will never [under any circumstances] desert you [nor give you up nor leave you without support, nor will I in any degree leave you helpless], nor will I forsake or let you down or relax My hold on you [assuredly not]!'" (Heb. 13:5 AMP).

Something supernatural happened through those words. The ache in my chest broke for a few hours. God gently drew me to his heart through my friend's reminder of God's indescribable, bottomless covenantal love for me—his *hesed*.

Slowly, God's love and sovereignty merged into a stunning tapestry filled with pictures of his past faithfulness and unbreakable promise of his eternal presence. Though still longing for Mark and all my shattered dreams, embers of his everlasting love fueled my journey and gave me strength to face each day with purpose.

When our sons asked what songs I wanted sung at Mark's memorial service, I requested "O, the Deep, Deep Love of Jesus!" Though we wanted to rejoice in our faith, I wanted a way to express the anguish and desperate need for Jesus in the coming days and this hymn, sung in a minor key, gave me hope. The words describe the very *hesed* Naomi experienced, yet they are far richer, because this deep, deep love flows from our Redeemer Jesus. May the message of *hesed* extended to us through the boundless love of Jesus lead us homeward, and may we flourish as we travel the path marked out for us by our God.

O the deep, deep love of Jesus! Vast, unmeasured,
       boundless, free;
rolling as a mighty ocean in its fullness over me.
Underneath me, all around me, is the current of thy
       love;
leading onward, leading homeward, to thy glorious rest
       above.

O the deep, deep love of Jesus! Spread his praise from
       shore to shore;
how he loveth, ever loveth, changeth never, nevermore;
how he watches o'er his loved ones, died to call them all
       his own;
how for them he intercedeth, watcheth o'er them from
       the throne.

O the deep, deep love of Jesus! Love of every love the
       best:
'tis an ocean vast of blessing, 'tis a haven sweet of rest.
O the deep, deep love of Jesus! 'Tis a heav'n of heav'ns
       to me;
and it lifts me up to glory, for it lifts me up to thee.

Judy's Story

Judy Didier has three children and nine grandchildren. She lives in Marietta, Georgia, where she serves on the Women's Ministry Committee of her church as coordinator of compassion ministries.

My mom had a plaque in her kitchen with the quote "Bloom Where You Are Planted!" I remembered these words when my husband left me after forty-three years of marriage. Could I recover from the shock of divorce and moving from the familiar to the unfamiliar? Could I ever bloom again? I took refuge in the Lord, and in the sanctuary of his presence, he ministered to me through his word, slowly breathing life, hope, and joy into my soul. Eventually he provided a new home and a loving church family who welcomed me.

I began to see his beauty all around me—birds singing, flowers blooming. He calls me to flourish and assures me it is possible: "Behold, I am doing a new thing; / now it springs forth, do you not perceive it? / I will make a way in the wilderness / and rivers in the desert" (Isa. 43:19).

My Lord has done more than I could ever hope or dream, but sometimes I allow my flesh to control my thoughts and actions. Then I must choose to remember and meditate on my Lord's words: "Whatever is true, whatever is honorable, whatever is just, whatever is pure, whatever is lovely, whatever is commendable, if there is any excellence, if there is anything worthy of praise, think about these things" (Phil. 4:8).

I praise the Lord for his faithfulness. He continually shows me in his word who he is. He shows me his love. He is my strength and protection. That is why I can never stop praising him; I declare his glory all day long (Ps. 71:7–8).

I ask him to let me proclaim his power to this new generation (Ps. 71:18). I want my children and grandchildren to know that in this broken world we will have troubles, but in Christ we can have joy, peace, contentment, and hope if we keep our eyes on him, surrender our will to his will, and flourish in his perfect plan for us.

Flourishing at this time in my life is resting in him, sitting with him, and hearing him speak to me from his word, lifting others up in prayer, smiling at others for him, giving a word of encouragement when he prompts, and being still in him. He is Jehovah-Jireh, my provider; Jehovah-Nissi, my banner; Jehovah-Rohi, my Shepherd. He is faithful to the end! I praise him and thank him!

Questions for Reflection and Discussion

1. How are you challenged to age with grace?

2. What does flourishing mean for you at this time in your life?

3. How will a better understanding of God's loyal, everlasting, unbreakable love for you change the way you view your present circumstances?

4. Pray Ephesians 3:14–21.

Concluding Thoughts

From Sharon

During a conversation with a friend who lost a son, I asked her, "Is it true God doesn't give us more than we can handle?" She laughed and responded, "No. And I'm living proof of that!"

Sadly, many of us face terrifying enemies believing God wants us to fight them on our own, because, after all, "He doesn't give us more than we can handle." Perhaps it takes growing old to recognize this statement as a lie. Aging with grace sometimes feels impossible. It is more than we can handle. Paul gave us a biblical perspective when he wrote: "We were so utterly burdened beyond our strength that we despaired of life itself. Indeed, we felt that we had received the sentence of death. But that was to make us rely not on ourselves but on God who raises the dead. . . . On him we have set our hope" (2 Cor. 1:8–10).

It's in those most broken places that we can learn to cry out: "We are powerless against this great horde that is coming against us. We do not know what to do, but our eyes are on you" (2 Chron. 20:12).

In 2011, Chuck had a widow-maker heart attack, and in 2016 he retired from pastoral ministry. A few months later he had brain surgery, which resulted in unexpected complications. Instead of going home as planned, we settled into a rehabilitation center where Chuck seemed to be in a semicomatose state. He later told me he felt imprisoned by a dark cloud, trapped between life and death.

As I watched over Chuck and prayed for him to come back to us, the Lord reminded me of the exciting days of serving alongside my husband in two inner-city churches where we learned to trust God for daily provision. I smiled at the memory of the six-year honeymoon we experienced when Chuck returned to our home church as a pastor, and I wept over the four years of church conflict that followed this idyllic time. Here I learned the meaning of lament. Then I remembered how God prepared a safe place for us in a church where everyone knew our warts but loved us anyway. A year later breast cancer threatened my life. During the months of intense chemotherapy God taught me what it means to receive his treasures in the darkness designed to turn my heart toward his love (Isa. 45:2–3). Four years later I clung to God's promise to send those treasures after the death of our son Mark.

Long-term grief taught me God is not afraid of my questions and he holds me tightly in his grip. Remembering God's past faithfulness when fear for Chuck overwhelmed me encouraged me to hold onto the hope and confidence that no matter the outcome, our God would not abandon us in that hospital waiting room. The surgery left Chuck with severe vertigo and loss of hearing in his left ear. Chuck's disabilities and other disappointments in this season of life drive us to our knees, where we cry out, "Lord, we don't know what to do, so our eyes are fixed on you." Though our journey is sometimes hard, we are grateful for the joy we experience every day through the many blessings the Lord pours over us.

Throughout this book, we have walked with biblical women whose confidence in God's promise of a Redeemer fueled their faith. We have also met contemporary women who cling to Jesus as they navigate the unexpected twists and turns in their last season of life. Because of their faith in the finished work of Jesus, each woman chooses, sometimes a thousand times a day, to believe she is part of God's bigger story and her life is about his glory.

I am grateful for women like these who cheer us on with this declaration: God is sovereign and we can trust him.

I pray the scriptural truths of this book help you flourish wherever you are in life's journey. Every time God gives you more than you can handle and the more powerless you feel, the deeper into the heart of God you can travel. Our Father is not afraid of your questions, and you are safely in his grip. Take some time away from the distractions of daily life and ask the Holy Spirit to open your mind and heart to God's word. Write out your fears and cry out to God for answers.

Ask God to remind you of his past faithfulness, and write a list of spiritual and physical blessings. Make a list of what torments and discourages you, and when you feel hopeless, pray, "Lord, I don't know what to do, so my eyes are fixed on you." Over each broken place choose to worship God with words similar to the prophet Habakkuk's prayer, and as you do, hear the voices of sisters from of old and across the world today, praying with you:

> Though the fig tree should not blossom,
>   nor fruit be on the vines,
> the produce of the olive fail
>   and the fields yield no food,
> the flock be cut off from the fold
>   and there be no herd in the stalls,
> yet I will rejoice in the Lord;
>   I will take joy in the God of my salvation.
>   (Hab. 3:17–18)

From Susan

Thank you for joining our quest to know what God's word says about glorifying him in old age. We have learned more than we had space to write, and there is more to learn until we fly away (Ps. 90:10) and faith becomes sight (2 Cor. 5:7). My sisters, wherever you are on life's timeline, begin now to pray for grace to finish strong, which means finishing weak.

Jesus said, "My grace is sufficient for you, for my power is made perfect in weakness." May our response be, "Therefore

I will boast all the more gladly of my weaknesses, so that the power of Christ may rest upon me. . . . When I am weak, then I am strong" (2 Cor. 12:9–10).

I knew this intellectually, but at age sixty-three I had a sudden and severe attack of vertigo that was eventually diagnosed as a virus in my inner ear. It caused total deafness in that ear and nerve damage that causes poor balance, so my body has to work hard to compensate, causing chronic weakness and fatigue. This abrupt change in my physical capacity helped me learn experientially the power and sweetness of weakness.

When my world started spinning wildly, I had no idea what was happening. I don't remember much about the next few days, but I vividly remember my first thought. I did not formulate it; it simply came—"Father, help me to welcome whatever you are bringing into my life." And there was peace, a stillness of soul. As I have reflected on that moment, I realize this thought came from deep within me. The Holy Spirit reminded me of everything I knew about God's love and sovereignty and encapsulated it in a response of faith. Since that time, as I wake each morning, I ask the Lord to give me grace to welcome whatever he brings into my life that day and strength to glorify him in it. Over the years there were times when this prayer became rote, but I continued.

And then, Sharon and I wrote this book. We were in our final editing phase before sending it to the publisher when I fell, and shortly after I recovered, Gene was hospitalized. As I write this, we are now at home with a caregiver to help me care for him. I'm tempted to ask, "Why did I write this book? Didn't I know the enemy would assault me with the ravages of aging?" But I am not willing to give Satan credit for the suffering of aging that Gene and I are experiencing. Daily God gives us grace to welcome what *he* sends. He gives us comfort through his presence and confidence in his promises. He makes us glad. This is a gladness that transcends our circumstances. Grief and gospel gladness can coexist, so I continually pray Psalm 86:3–4: "Be gracious to me, O Lord. . . . / *Gladden* the soul of your servant, / for to you, O Lord, do I lift up my soul."

As our friend Pastor George Grant wrote us, "These frail frames are reminding us that we are meant for the renewal of all things in the new heavens and new earth! Rest in his provision. Trust in his providence. Walk in his mercy. Remain in his love. Rely on his strength. Stand fast."

So don't fight or deny your weakness. Instead, let it bring a childlike dependence upon our Father, who tells us:

> Listen to me, O house of Jacob, . . .
> who have been borne by me from before your birth,
>   carried from the womb;
> even to your old age, I am he,
>   and to gray hairs I will carry you. (Isa. 46:3–4)

This lovely imagery expresses how I feel about being an old lady. I feel like a tired, dependent, glad, and grateful little girl being carried in the arms of her Father, calling to her friends,

"Look how good and strong my daddy is!" And she knows that when she falls asleep in his arms, she'll wake up at home and will "dwell in the house of the LORD forever" (Ps. 23:6).

I often pray the prayer from the hymn "O Sacred Head, Now Wounded": "O make me thine forever; and should I fainting be, Lord, let me never, never outlive my love to thee."[1]

That's my prayer, but my comfort and confidence is that even if my mental faculties fade and I forget my love for Jesus, I will never, never outlive his love for me. So dear sister, let's join generations of flourishing ones who preceded us and confess our faith:

Westminster Shorter Catechism

Q. 1. What is the chief end of man?

Man's chief end is to glorify God, and to enjoy him for ever.

Q. 2. What rule hath God given to direct us how we may glorify and enjoy him?

The word of God, which is contained in the Scriptures of the Old and New Testaments, is the only rule to direct us how we may glorify and enjoy him.

Heidelberg Catechism

Q. 1. What is your only comfort in life and in death?

That I am not my own, but belong—body and soul, in life and in death—to my faithful Savior Jesus Christ.

---

1   Bernard of Clairvaux, "O Sacred Head, Now Wounded."

He has fully paid for all my sins with his precious blood, and has set me free from the tyranny of the devil. He also watches over me in such a way that not a hair can fall from my head without the will of my Father in heaven; in fact, all things must work together for my salvation. Because I belong to him, Christ, by his Holy Spirit, assures me of eternal life and makes me wholeheartedly willing and ready from now on to live for him.

General Index

Scripture Index

Aging with Grace
Leader's Guide

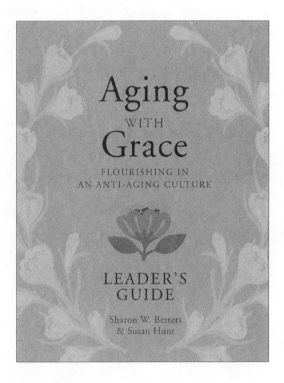

Focusing on prayer, community, and Bible study, Sharon and Susan
guide readers through all eight chapters of *Aging with Grace* in a format
suitable for group study. Each lesson includes a preparation section with
ideas for the entire group, a lesson plan for the teacher, and a handout
to be copied and distributed.

Available online at **pcabookstore.com** or by phone at 1 (800) 283-1357.

Also Available from Susan Hunt

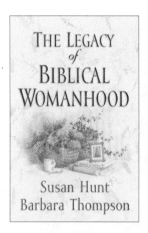

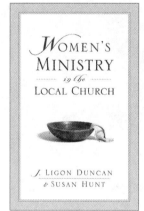

For more information, visit **crossway.org**.